Michigan 48603

The Hidden Skier

Corky Fowler and Christopher Smith

cbi Contemporary Books, Inc.
Chicago

Library of Congress Cataloging in Publication Data

Fowler, Corky,
    The hidden skier.

    1. Skis and skiing.   2. Sports—Psychological
aspects.   I. Smith, Christopher, 1944-
joint author.   II. Title.
GV854.F68   1977   796.9'3   77-75722
ISBN 0-8092-7900-2

Photography and drawings by SHERRY FOWLER

Promotional consideration SNOWBIRD CORPORATION
SUN VALLEY COMPANY
K2 SKI CORPORATION
SCOTT USA

Published by Contemporary Books, Inc.
180 North Michigan Avenue, Chicago, Illinois 60601
Manufactured in the United States of America
Library of Congress Catalog Card Number:77-75722
International Standard Book Number: 0-8092-7900-2

Published simultaneously in Canada by
Beaverbooks
953 Dillingham Road
Pickering, Ontario L1W 1Z7
Canada

It would be difficult to thank any one person for his or her contribution to this book. Truthfully, everyone we know has contributed in his own way.

We could probably fill three pages telling you how we feel about writing this book, and it all would be saying, "thank you, we love you," to everyone we know.

So, thank you, we love you.

Table of Contents

Preface

This is not a "how to" book. It is a book about our experiences in learning to ski. We have written this book to share two things we enjoy enormously: the joy of skiing and the continuing process of discovering our hidden talents.

The book is a guide for you to use in your own development as a skier. We have seen that people learn quickly and enjoy themselves when they learn through their own process of self-discovery. When you discover something in skiing for yourself, it becomes your own. We have used this observation as a guiding principle in writing this book.

We are presenting experiences, processes, and fundamentals that we have found workable in becoming accomplished skiers. We discovered these things through reviewing our personal skiing careers, our experiences while conducting the Hidden Athlete Workshops, and through observing the careers of other accomplished skiers. What we discovered has worked and continues to work for us, and we know it can work for you.

Introduction
by Corky Fowler

INTRODUCTION

I fell in love with skiing when I was a teenager. It was one of the first activities of my life in which I experienced personal freedom and tasted my potential abilities. Through skiing, I defined a purpose and a goal for myself; I was very certain about where I wanted to go and what I wanted to accomplish. I wanted to be a professional skier, traveling around the world, meeting people from all walks of life, and getting paid for it. But, above all, I just wanted to ski because I really loved to do it!

Since then, I have skied in the U.S.A., Canada, South America, Japan, Western Europe, Iran, and New Zealand. I have met many people, from astronauts to janitors and bartenders and millionaires. And I've gotten paid for it! I was extremely successful at all aspects of what I set out to do, except for one. I lost the experience of loving what I was doing.

Three years ago as I was skiing on a beautiful, sunny day at Snowbird, I suddenly realized that I wasn't enjoying myself. Here I was in the middle of one of the most famous and beautiful resorts in the world, doing what many people would give up everything to do, and I wasn't having any fun. The more I studied my situation, the more I saw that the "fun" had been slowly disappearing not only from skiing but from other areas of my life as well. I knew that skiing had not changed (the mountains and the snow were still the same), but my experience of skiing had somehow altered.

What I really wanted was simply to have fun. I was doing all the things that symbolized having fun, but I wasn't enjoying myself. I decided to begin a process of looking within myself to find out why I no longer enjoyed skiing, the one thing in life in which I had always found immense joy and pleasure. It was not easy to take the journey inward, but I felt that the only path to finding the answers was to look within and see what I was doing to keep myself from enjoying life.

I found it difficult to tell the truth about my feelings, usually because the truth seemed ridiculous. Or perhaps I didn't like to hear the truth because it was different from what I wanted it to be. I have since recognized that telling the truth about my feelings is the key to personal freedom and greater self-acceptance. Through the recognition of my true feelings, my inner and outer conflicts subside, and I experience more freedom and joy in skiing as well as in all of life.

It was only fitting that I met and began working on this book with Chris Smith. His background in education, sports, and personal exploration is similar to, and yet different from, my own. He is very interested in and curious about people and has a highly unusual and well-developed talent for working with people in teaching and learning situations. His abilities to probe the inner self and his support of people have been key factors in the creation of this book.

Neither of us had written a book before, and truthfully, we were nervous when we started. But we knew that we had something to say,

INTRODUCTION

and we wanted to create a book that would make skiing easier and more fun for anyone. At first, we found that we weren't able to put our thoughts down on paper. We began by writing down all the things that sounded impressive—the good, esoteric, vague, philosophical stuff that we heard people talking about. After two months of writing, we stopped and looked at what we had written. It was nonsense.

That discovery was a valuable lesson. We had both learned in skiing that the more we were willing to trust ourselves, the more our innate athletic abilities worked for us and produced better and easier skiing. But we didn't transfer that knowledge to the process of writing this book! We weren't drawing from our own personal experiences in sports and teaching. Crazy as it sounds, we had been writing without trusting ourselves. As soon as we began trusting ourselves, the writing began to flow. We saw what it was that we wanted to say and realized that both of us had many valuable experiences in learning and teaching skiing that were worth sharing.

Once we started writing, though, another problem appeared. I found it exceedingly difficult to share my experiences about skiing. I felt torn between two powerful forces within myself—a part that wanted to write, another that did not. I discovered a strong belief within me that said, "If I really tell people what I know about skiing, someone will be able to ski better than I do; then my friends won't appreciate me for being so good." I realized that I thought I had to be the best in whatever I did for people to like me.

INTRODUCTION

The mystery about why I wasn't having fun began to unravel. I was so busy trying to be better than everyone else that I'd lost the experience of just sliding down the mountain. I recognized that when I am concerned about **being better,** or **looking good all the time,** or **winning all the time above all else,** I lose the simple joy of doing what I am doing. Now I find that a major source of fun in my life is sharing myself with others. Can you imagine being an actor without an audience? Or a tennis player without an opponent? Or a skier without anyone to share the beauty and joy of skiing? That would be dull!

The processes, exercises, and attitudes presented in this book have been used successfully in the Hidden Athlete Workshop. The workshop is the living version of this book. We have seen that people are able to apply these same things in all sports. The success of these processes, exercises, and attitudes have been demonstrated to us by people of all ages and ability levels who have participated in the workshop throughout the western states. We don't ask you to believe them—try them out for yourself. It is through your own experience that you learn to ski. You are your own greatest teacher.

During our careers in teaching and skiing, there have been occasions when we have been tempted to stress mental awareness over physical activity and vice versa. We recognize that it is impossible to insist that one is more important than the other. They are equally important. It is true that we must have our thoughts in line with what we wish to achieve physically or we will experience difficulty in our

INTRODUCTION

physical activities. It is also true that things do not happen in the physical world without our physically doing them. Sitting around and thinking won't make them happen.

Though you will have to translate the process, exercises, and attitudes presented in this book into physical action, we want you to know that you can do anything you want in skiing. You are incredibly talented, though you may not believe it or experience it right now. We are behind you one hundred percent in your pursuit of discovering and having fun with your amazing hidden talents.

Finally, we recognize that it's not necessary to be an Olympic champion in order to have fun with skiing. Simply accomplishing whatever goals you may have as a skier, allowing yourself to be foolish sometimes, and enjoying the beauty of winter will provide all the fun possible in skiing. The fun in skiing is, simply, the thrill of doing it.

1

Athletic Performance and the Mind

As I continue to work with people, I see that the level of ability experienced by each person is intricately connected to how much ability he thinks he has. People who think that they are capable learn more quickly and easily than people who feel they are incapable. I hear nothing but "I can" from fast learners. From slower learners, I continually hear things such as: "It's hard to learn new things at my age"; "I'm really not a very physical person"; or "Skiing is really a hard sport to learn." There is always a negative attitude present in slow learners.

Everyone's body contains some amount of strength and has the natural capacity to perform exceptionally coordinated physical movements. Our bodies are capable of being very efficient. How many of us even notice all of the physical skills we perform every day? We take walking, eating, and talking for granted, yet we certainly didn't take these things for granted when we first attempted to do them. Look closely at talking or eating, for example, and you will see how much coordination is required between the different muscle groups to make everything work smoothly. After we have learned these movements, we take them for granted and forget how much work and time we put into learning them.

Children are very free about learning. Watch any child when he is first learning how to eat with a fork and knife. His food is on the table, on the floor, and on his face. Yet, eventually all children become proficient at performing eating movements. In fact, rarely does anyone consider that a child will not become proficient. The truth is that children do not question their ability to do something; they go ahead and do it.

When I work with children, I rarely hear any of them say "I can't." With adults, it's a different story. I continually hear "I can't." When I am teaching children, I don't explain how to do anything. I just say, "Where would you like to ski?" or "Let's ski all the way to the bottom," or "Make sure you are comfortable when you do anything on skis." I give them challenges that will allow them to discover that skiing is fun and easy. They rarely ask me how to do anything. Adults are different. The first question they usually ask is, "How do I do this?" Adults want to understand how to do it "right." Children are completely unconcerned with understanding how they do things; they are only interested in doing them and having fun.

I am struck by the marked difference between the speed at which the majority of children learn and the speed at which the majority of adults learn. Children are running circles around adults while the adults are "figuring out" what to do.

As young children we don't know how we are supposed to look as skiers, so we ski in whatever way is natural for us. Our rhythms are easy and our bodies learn from experience. As we get older, we learn how a skier should look; then we try to look like that, instead of like ourselves. Our learning process becomes forced rather than natural. If we believe that there is a "way" to look as a skier, we will try to ski like that, even though it may not feel comfortable and natural to us.

In this way, we set ourselves up for that old judgment game called "Do I look all right?" The process is continuous and, for the most part, unconscious. It's that little voice in our head telling us what we are doing, how we are doing, and what everyone else will think about it. It's our thoughts, measuring us, explaining us to us, and rationalizing everything for us. We're defining who we are. We are being our ultimate judge, usually the most demanding one in our world.

We create our self-image, our own separate reality, through this process. We tell ourselves when we are succeeding and when we are failing. We tell ourselves how capable we are. Our expectations as to how well we are able to ski are based on how much talent and ability we see in ourselves. All of our physical performances are in tune with our expectations. For example, as a skier, if I have progressed slowly for the past five years, does that mean that I will have to progress slowly for the next five years? It does not. Yet if I believe that I have progressed slowly because of my lack of athletic ability, and if I think that people without much ability learn slowly, then for the next five years I will probably produce a like performance; I will expect nothing more of myself. Conversely, if I have progressed in leaps and bounds during the last five years, I will expect to continue progressing at that rate.

The situation we face is that our memory stores all of our opinions and expectations of ourselves. Our minds automatically produce a reaction, one linked to the past, when faced with a like situation in the present. Since there is something in every new situation that we can relate to the past, we deal with new situations by using past reactions. It's like a circle; if I ski poorly in the bumps, I form the opinion that I ski poorly in the bumps. Each time I approach any bumps, I remember immediately how poorly I did the last time. I approach them anticipating the same performance. As soon as I make one slip, which I inevitably will do, I immediately say to myself: "I knew it! It's the same thing every time. Am I ever going to learn to ski the bumps?" Now I have successfully added one more experience as proof of my inability to ski the bumps.

We can get so caught up in seeing what we do poorly that we often miss what we do well. Perhaps the most common example in my experience of teaching is the person who will not acknowledge any skill he does have. I saw how ridiculous that was as person after person refused my compliments. They would be skiing quite well and would not see the obvious. They had to look like champions to be acceptable. That type of self-imposed criticism can only take the fun out of skiing. What are our chances of improving or having fun with skiing, if we continually see faults in ourselves and in our performance? It's crazy.

Now when I encounter a student like this, I ask him: "Can you do anything on skis? Can you stop; can you turn; can you ski fast; can you jump off a bump, etc., etc.?" If he tries to tell me how bad he is, I remind him that he is not answering the question. Eventually, he will see that he can do quite a bit as a skier; his only real problem is that he doesn't look like last year's world champion, and he thinks he should because he's been skiing for almost three years now.

If you are constantly aware of everything you do wrong when you ski, or if you find that skiing is hard work for you, try this exercise.

> *Go skiing and, for a couple of hours, let your body take care of itself. Let it do whatever it wants to do. Be foolish. Forget about where your poles should go or how you should be bending your knees. Ski fast or slow, whatever you like, but just continue skiing without stopping. Let yourself go!*

I have found this exercise to be one of the most valuable of them all.

It is fun and challenging to go out and ski without stopping, other than for lifts or short rests. There's no time to analyze "rights" and "wrongs." For anyone caught up in trying to ski "right," skiing long distances, nonstop, without any regard for form, will do wonders for his skiing.

For the most part, it is our undermining and negative thoughts that keep us from reaching our desired level of skiing. Those thoughts come in all forms, sizes, and shapes. They can be created as easily by the things we see, hear, or read about as they can by our actual experience on skis.

Skiing, like all sports, is loaded with common misconceptions. Experienced skiers, ski instructors, racers, lift operators, etc., pass notions on to new skiers who are hungry for any information that might help them. Beginning skiers have no experience with which to evaluate the information; therefore, the natural thing for them to do is to accept it.

When I first started skiing I was told that: (1) Skiing in the powder was dangerous; I could get hurt easily; (2) I could expect to get hurt at least once every five years; it was unavoidable; (3) If I really cared about improving my skiing, I would ski every day possible; and (4) The women would go wild over me when I could ski well.

I have since found that not one of those beliefs has ever been true, and regrettably, even the women haven't gone wild over me. Yet, for at least a year and a half, I was apprehensive about skiing in powder. I can remember saying to myself, "Be careful, you're going into the powder now; don't get hurt." After four years, I finally gave up wondering when I was going to get hurt. And, after one full season, I finally stopped feeling guilty for not skiing every day. I realize now that the beliefs I had originated from the opinions of other people. I accepted them without reservation, even though I had no personal experience with their particular opinions.

Often I will discover a belief that I have not been aware of even having. For example, a few years back, I believed that you needed very short skis to ski well in the moguls. Freestyle skiing was flourishing; everyone was talking about the quickness of short skis, and several magazine articles appeared proclaiming the success of short skis in mogul skiing. I actually began to believe that I could not ski well in the moguls on my own skis because they were 205 cm. and they were slow in turning when compared to a shorter ski. I would fall and, without hesitation, blame it on my longer skis. I began to resent my skis and started believing that, because they were long, I was going to have problems in the moguls. The more I knew I was going to have problems, the more problems I had. My mogul skiing began to suffer, and I started losing my confidence. It seemed that the only solution was to buy shorter skis.

Just before I bought them, I had a day of skiing with a friend of mine, Don Orrell, an accomplished skier who loved to race. He was skiing for fun that day on his 215 cm. downhill skis (exceptionally long skis!) I was skiing behind Don, when at one point, he began making a series of quick-linked turns. I could not believe how fast his skis were turning! I tried to ski in rhythm, making the same number of turns, but I could not do it. And my skis were 10 cm. shorter! I was stunned! I did not believe that it was possible to make turns that fast unless one had short skis. After seeing Don, though, my first thought was, "If he can make quick turns, so can I."

I stopped blaming my skis for my problems in the moguls and realized that I could turn any ski quickly. I started concentrating on making quicker turns, especially in the moguls. It worked! My mogul skiing began to improve. Now when I read or hear an opinion, I accept it, but only as that person's opinion, not as mine. I'll look into my own experience and see if it is true for me. If I have no experience concerning the subject, I'll wait until my own experience helps me formulate an opinion.

Have you heard and do you agree with any of the following common beliefs about skiing? (1) Women can't ski as well as men; (2) Powder is more difficult to ski than hard pack; (3) Skiing among the trees is dangerous; (4) You need to start skiing at a very young age to be able to ski well; or (5) You need to be in super physical condition to ski well. If you agree with any of these, you have just discovered a belief that could be limiting you.

As I continue working with people, I realize that whatever beliefs they may have about themselves completely dominate their performance. The positive beliefs encourage them, and the negative ones act as barriers that keep them from achieving what they desire.

Everyone has the natural ability to ski anywhere on the mountain that he chooses. By aligning thoughts in a positive way, anyone can experience that ability and become an accomplished skier.

2

Improving Your Skiing Through Your Thoughts

One of the most powerful tools you can use to improve your skiing is your mind. Something I continually see among accomplished athletes in all sports is that those who constantly see their capability experience it. They don't concern themselves with thinking about their setbacks or initial failures. They align their thoughts in a positive way, a way that envisions success.

When I first began skiing, the biggest problem I had to contend with was my embarrassment. I would do anything to avoid looking bad. After three full seasons of skiing, I was still telling people, "I'm just learning, I'm really not very good." I knew that, if they thought I was a beginner, they wouldn't expect me to look very good; then I might surprise them with a couple of good turns. If they said, "Hey, you're pretty good!" I would deny it immediately.

I had conflicting feelings, however. I really wanted to tell people I was a good skier, yet I knew that if I did, I would feel as if I always had to look good and I was afraid that I wouldn't. Labeling myself a beginner was an uncomfortable feeling, but at least I was safe from my own and other people's judgments.

One day, someone finally said: "When are you going to give up that 'I'm just learning' line? You'll always be learning. Why don't you have some fun and stop judging yourself all of the time. What's the point? You ski pretty well, start noticing that."

As I listened to him, I felt a little embarrassed at how accurately he had seen me. I also recognized that he had given me some pretty good advice. I began to look at all of the things I could do on skis. I was surprised at how much I knew. The more I saw my ability, the easier it became to imagine myself getting better and better. Skiing became easier and I was having more fun; I even stopped telling people that I was just learning. I changed my attention from what I wasn't able to do to what I could do and wanted to do. I also accepted the awkwardness I felt at times as being okay.

As I began teaching, I noticed that most of my students did what I had done. They were more aware of their faults than of their strong points and the things they could do well. Instead of asking me with a smile, "How am I doing?" they would get very serious and say, "What am I doing wrong?" I would answer, "Nothing." It never satisfied them. They would say, "I know I must be doing *something* wrong." I finally began working with their thoughts and attitudes as well as with their skiing just as I had done with myself.

What had worked for me also worked for my students. Skiing became easier, and the learning process was more fun for them.

The Power of Thoughts

The effect our thoughts have upon us is enormous. When we focus our attention on a specific thought, we create a flow of energy in that direction. The more we continue to focus on that thought, the more energy we put into its direction. As our energy grows, we feel more certain about our course. Achieving what we are after becomes a matter of simply doing whatever we need to do to stay in line with our thoughts.

A simple example would be: I decide I will play tennis. I get in my car and go to the tennis courts. I find out there is a citywide tournament going on and most of the courts will not be free. It would take some looking to find an open court. I can go home and play tennis some other time, or I can look for an open court. I really want to play tennis. I get in my car and decide to drive until I find an open court. Forty-five minutes later I find one. I find someone to play with and play for two hours. I'm happy.

By keeping my attention on wanting to play tennis, I gave myself the necessary energy and direction that I needed to find an open court so I could play tennis.

There are two types of thoughts on which we can focus our attention: positive or negative ones. Whichever choice we make will have a dramatic effect upon our performance.

Successful athletes constantly use the power of their positive thoughts. Their thoughts serve as guidelines for their physical experience.

> Focusing Your Attention on Positive Thoughts Is the Key Factor in Becoming an Accomplished Skier

To experience the different effects that you have in your body when you are focusing on a negative or a positive thought, do these two exercises.

> *(1)   Take thirty to forty seconds and imagine yourself doing something physical that you know you can do well. Tell yourself how easy it is for you to do this particular thing.*

What did you see and feel during the exercise? You probably felt relaxed and saw a smooth performance.

> *(2)   Take another thirty to forty seconds and imagine yourself doing something physical that you feel unsure about—something that you really don't trust yourself to do well. Tell yourself how difficult this is for you.*

What did you see and feel in that exercise? Did you notice the tightening of your muscles and any other related body reaction?

When I feel unsure of myself, my body reacts. My muscles become tense, and whatever I am doing becomes an effort. The obvious effect, of course, shows in my performance. My chances of succeeding in what I'm doing diminish and I lose confidence. My tension increases. If anybody is watching, I become embarrassed and, consequently, even more tense. I create a vicious circle for myself, with the end result being that I interrupt my natural muscle flow and I can't perform up to my ability.

There may be times when you feel unsure of yourself. That alone will not have any dramatic effect on your skiing. There *will* be an effect, though, if you continue to focus your attention on your negative feelings. You'll interfere with your natural movements.

Locating and Neutralizing Your Negative Thoughts

Regardless of your performance as a skier, you can enrich your experience of skiing and raise your level of ability when you neutralize the negative thoughts you have with positive thoughts.

> To Successfully Neutralize a Negative Thought, You Need to Focus Your Attention on the Opposite Positive Thought

For example, if you hear a little voice in your head repeatedly telling you that you are weak and clumsy when you ski in the moguls, you are focusing your attention on a negative thought. To successfully neutralize that thought, you need to consciously rechannel your thoughts in the opposite, positive direction. That is, at the same time that thought appears, tell yourself something like: "I'm not listening to you, thought, you're not worth hearing. I know if I just continue to ski in the moguls I will improve."

The principal strength in the process of neutralizing a thought lies in your continuing to create the opposite thought until the negative one either disappears or you recognize that it is a "leftover" reaction without any meaning. Don't set a time limit for this to happen, just continue focusing until it does.

I can relate an experience from my own skiing in which I was able to effect a dramatic change in what I was able to do by taking my attention off my negative thoughts and refocusing it on positive thoughts. A few years back when I began skiing longer distances at much faster speeds, I found that my leg muscles always became tired after a short distance. I thought perhaps I wasn't strong enough, so I began running and conditioning, determined to increase my strength. It didn't work. I continued thinking I wasn't strong enough. I thought maybe if I relaxed more I could save some of my strength. I tried it and found that I couldn't ski well because I was trying to figure out how to relax and ski at the same time. My conditioning wasn't working, nor was anything else. I felt defeated. Every time I faced a long run, I'd say to myself, "Get ready, this is going to be a real effort."

There was a friend of mine who also skied long runs, only she never became tired. I asked her how she did it. She said matter-of-factly, "I don't think about getting tired. I think about how easy the run will be."

"You really never get tired?" I said, unbelieving.

She answered, "Yes, occasionally, but I immediately tell myself it will go away and that it's really an easy run. That seems to work."

I tried it. Just before skiing a long run I'd say to myself, "This run will be easy. I'll float over the snow. I'll let my skis do all the work, and I won't get tired at all." Initially I still became tired, but I told myself that the tiredness would disappear, maybe not this run, but I would eventually stop becoming tired. It began to work! I was able to ski farther and farther without feeling tired. My skiing improved! I felt myself relaxing more and thinking about how far I could ski rather than how much of an effort it would be.

I began applying my thinking to other areas of my skiing and found it worked there too. It was exciting. I felt as though I had found some magical way within myself to improve my skiing. I shared my experience with several friends and found that it was as magical and workable for them also.

In this example, I discovered that the belief I had about my body not being strong enough to ski long distances was a negative belief, and mentally I was holding myself back, although I was not aware of it at the time.

There could be several negative thoughts in your mind that you may not recognize. Once you are aware of them, they can be neutralized.

> If You Know What Your Negative Thoughts Are, You Can Neutralize Them.

Here is an exercise that will help you find out how you really feel about yourself as a skier.

Take a pen and a piece of paper and give yourself two minutes to answer this question: **"Why can't I ski well?"**

Write down the first reactions that enter your mind. Don't think about whether they are right or wrong and keep writing for the full two minutes.

Now take two more minutes to answer this question: **"Why can I ski really well?"**

Again, write down all of your thoughts for the full two minutes.

Go over both of your lists when you have finished.

Through the exercises, you will clearly see your negative thoughts. You will also find out how capable you think you are. Once you recognize these negative thoughts, there are two methods that you can use to neutralize them. One way is to focus your attention on the appropriate positive thought for three or four minutes at a time. Use any free moment—when you are riding up a chair lift, driving your car, or taking a walk, etc. What you are doing is simply creating a positive flow of energy which will counteract the negative thought.

The other method is to create opposite positive thoughts *as* you are experiencing negative reactions. You cannot stop your mind from reacting; it's automatic and natural. You *can* neutralize its effects, though, by creating opposite positive thoughts at the same time that you are reacting negatively.

Both methods work well.

Skiing in Your Mind

There are two ways in which you can effectively improve your skiing through your thoughts. One is to neutralize negative thoughts about yourself as a skier, and the other is to use your imagination in a creative way and "Ski in your mind."

Skiing in your mind is imagining yourself skiing the way you want to ski. You can create yourself skiing any way you would like. You can do flips; ski in between moguls; float through deep powder; or ski in slow motion and feel the snow underneath your skis. The value in doing this is that you have the opportunity to become familiar with skiing movements without ever going out on the snow and you can ski any time of the year.

Here is a specific method of focusing my attention that I use when I ski in my mind. I choose an aspect of my skiing that I would like to improve upon. Perhaps it is turning in the powder. I then see myself making only powder turns for three to five minutes. If any other thoughts should enter my mind, I immediately refocus on my powder turns. I do this exercise three or four times a week, focusing my attention on the same thought. Through this one exercise, I have noticeably improved several aspects of my skiing.

I've been mentally practicing my skiing during the summers for years. On the first day of each ski season, I ski as well as I did on the last day of the past season. Before I began mentally skiing, it would usually take me several days to be able to ski as well as I had the year before.

"Skiing in your mind" is an extremely effective method of creating positive results in your skiing. In the chapter on Becoming an Accomplished Skier we mention "skiing in your mind" once again because we have experienced it to be one of the single most valuable tools for improving anyone's skiing.

3

Being Yourself When You Ski

23

BEING YOURSELF WHEN YOU SKI

As important as your mind is in your learning process, the kinds of things you do when you ski are just as important. The combination of the two is what determines how fast you will improve your skiing and how accomplished you can ultimately become.

So how do you find out what you should do on the snow? There are probably several ways you could find out, including just putting on the skis, taking the lift to the top of the mountain, and making it to the bottom. Most of us, though, use teachers, either in the form of a friend or a professional.

Skiing becomes very interesting at this point. It can also become very confusing. The first thing you are told is "how to ski," that is, "Do this; don't do that." You find out immediately that there are certain things you are not supposed to do. Since you are usually somewhat worried about how you are going to stop yourself from sliding all the way to the bottom completely out of control, you gladly accept anything anyone tells you. The problem is that there is no way of even knowing if what you are being told is correct. Have you ever noticed how well some of the people ski who are telling their friends how to ski? Sometimes it's difficult to tell who is leading whom.

If you are a new skier, the real difficulty at this stage is that your mind becomes so filled with ideas and beliefs about what you should or shouldn't do that you aren't learning to ski. You are just trying to make sure you don't do anything wrong. What can be more frustrating is that you are often told conflicting ideas about what is right!

In my own experience, I found that the more I tried to understand all of the things I was supposed to do to accomplish a certain movement, the more difficult that movement became for me to do. Understanding the movement was easy, I could get that. The problem came when I tried to do the movement. I would always be thinking about what I should be doing, to make sure that I did it right, at the same time that I was trying to do it. It never worked.

I can recall an experience in my first year of skiing that illustrates this situation perfectly. I was trying to learn a new way to turn over the top of a mogul and a friend, Jim, had given me perfect "how to do it" instructions. I memorized his instructions word for word.

I had the turn all figured out. "If I plant my pole in exactly the right place and bend my knees at precisely the same time I'm planting my pole, I will set up the turn perfectly. I need to make sure my wrist is turned slightly outward while I'm planting my pole; I don't want to miss the plant. Then, I lean into the turn, bring my other arm around, drive it down toward the fall line, let the bump gently push my knees up so I can absorb it perfectly, press my knees into the turn, turn my outside foot into the turn, push my toes down, transfer my weight to my downhill ski, let my legs unfold into the turn, and, above all, stay relaxed. The beauty of this turn is that it will happen naturally."

BEING YOURSELF WHEN YOU SKI

After getting this all straight in my mind, I headed for the bump, thinking of the pole plant. I remember it clearly; I planted the pole and promptly tripped over it. I tried again, and this time I was going so slow that I stopped halfway through the turn and fell over. I tried several more times and was not able to succeed at it. I could not understand what had happened. I quit in disgust and skied home feeling like a failure.

The next day I was skiing, not thinking about anything, when suddenly I did the turn in the middle of a bump run. It happened by itself. I continued skiing in the bumps and more and more turns materialized.

I realized that, the day before, I had been so determined to understand the turn and make it in the "right way" that I had not allowed myself to look any other way. My body was severely restricted and became stiff because it had not been allowed any room for error. I had the picture in my head, but I had tried to look at the picture at the same time as I was attempting to do the turn. I recognized that I could not successfully do something at the same time that I was thinking about it. I succeeded the next day because I took the pressure off myself by letting myself ski as me, not as Jim. I had already spent time focusing my attention on the turn. I knew what I wanted to do. I let it happen by itself in its own time.

There Is No Right Way to Ski

One of the greatest blocks to skiing naturally is the false assumption that there is a single "right way" to ski. If that were true, then all great skiers, past and present, would ski exactly the same way.

There are certain basic elements in skiing that need to be observed if we want to become very accomplished skiers, yet there is a great deal of room for each of us to develop our own style and still use these basic elements.

I had seen the style of my friend Jim, who was teaching me the turn. He was using the basic elements that were necessary for the turn to work, but as he described the turn he told me how *he* did it. He *didn't* tell me the elements of the turn. It did not occur to me that I could look different from him and still successfully do the turn. The more I tried to look like Jim, the more I stopped my own natural movements from taking place. I wasn't looking at the elements of the turn; I was looking at what Jim was doing. He kept telling me to do what *he* was doing, instead of letting me find what was natural for me within the basic elements of the turn.

When I stopped trying to do the turn in exactly the right way, I could let my body ski naturally. I kept the picture of Jim making the turn in my mind so that I had a workable model of the turn to use as a guide. As long as I didn't force myself to look exactly the same as

Jim, my own uniqueness and individual style continued to develop as I learned the turn.

There Is No Right Way to Look

A great injustice many skiers do to themselves is to assume that they haven't learned to ski yet because they don't look like the instructor, or the person everyone agrees is a good skier.

There is an attitude that continually surfaces among the people I work with. I had that same attitude myself in the first three or four years of my own skiing. That is, I wouldn't call myself a skier until I looked like an accomplished skier. I'd say things like, "I ski, but not really very well," or "I've only skied for two seasons—I'm not what you would really call a skier yet." I was embarrassed to say that I was a skier because I knew I wasn't very accomplished.

In the situation that I just described I was focusing my attention on my *lack* of ability. I wasn't looking at myself as a skier, but as something less than that. The most humorous aspect of the whole thing was: here I was skiing, yet I wouldn't call myself a skier!

I can choose to go around believing that I'm not a skier because I'm not very accomplished, or I can recognize that everyone on the mountain is a skier no matter what they look like, and at the same time some are going to be more accomplished than others. There is no "one way to look" to be a skier. If I should be at a stage at which I cannot ski powder or bumps very well, I am still a skier. I just don't ski powder and bumps very well, that's all.

Ski for Yourself

Somewhere along the way, I reached the point at which I skied just to ski and did not have to ski perfectly and at that time, my experience of skiing completely changed. I was free to be me. I had much more fun, and unexpectedly, my skiing improved immensely.

This is not to say that I disregarded technique. What I did was to use a workable technique, such as what my friend Jim demonstrated to me, as a guideline. Within that guideline, I drew upon my own experience to tell me what particular movements felt most comfortable for me. For example, both Jim and I carry our poles in front of us. That is the established technique, yet I have my poles four inches lower than Jim's. That is the difference between our personal styles. That is what is most natural for each of us.

It's for each of us to experiment and find the movements that work best. Sometimes we may look different from the accomplished skier, but if what we are doing is successful for us, we should continue doing it.

BEING YOURSELF WHEN YOU SKI

Established technique is for us to use as a starting point. We don't have to hold ourselves to looking any certain way. Accomplished skiers continually innovate within their own styles. That's why established techniques continually change over the years. Olympic champions of the 1950s do not look like the Olympic champions of the 1970s. They all use the same basic elements in their skiing, yet the newer champions, through constant innovations, both in their equipment and in their personal styles, have found more efficient ways to move their bodies.

Teachers, coaches, and other observers record the more efficient movements that the most successful skiers make, and those movements become incorporated into the latest technique. Then we as skiers, wanting to improve our skiing, have the most efficient model available to us to serve as a guide.

The beauty of technique is that anyone is free to innovate within it. You aren't bound by it. It's for you to experiment with your own movements to find out how you can best succeed as a skier.

4

The Basic Elements
of Skiing

THE BASIC ELEMENTS OF SKIING

A few years ago I saw that there were basic elements in skiing that were shared by all skiers, regardless of their nationality. I also recognized that **all of the national and international techniques of skiing are simply different interpretations of movement based on the same laws of nature.**

The value of knowing about the similarities in all techniques is that it greatly simplifies skiing for anyone. When I became clear about the basic elements in skiing, I was able to make *any* technical system work for me. Eventually I started borrowing the workable things I found in all techniques and began to create a way of skiing that was uniquely my own.

What I am presenting here are those basic elements that I see as the foundation of all techniques. Using these elements in your own skiing will help you create your own style—a style that will be based soundly upon the elementary laws of nature.

These elements are:

    A. Natural Balance
    B. The Use of Gravity
    C. Efficient Movement
    D. Harmonizing with the Terrain
    E. The Anatomy of a Ski

Natural Balance

Natural balance is the ability we all have to stay on our feet while skiing, or, even more simply, the ability to stand up. This form of balance is what works best while skiing, that is, letting the body dictate the best stance for maintaining balance.

I spent four winters trying to teach people how to traverse by having them assume a predetermined "traverse position." The results were people traversing on skis who looked like cigar store Indians. They were unable to traverse effectively. Finally, in frustration, I asked myself, "What is the purpose of a traverse?" The purpose is to cross a slope without losing altitude, and it is achieved by standing or balancing on the edges of the skis while crossing the slope. I decided to let the students do the work. I asked people to do whatever was necessary to stand on the edges of the skis while they traversed across the hill. People responded by creating beautiful, effective traverses! The lesson for me was that everyone has the ability to balance on skis naturally, without positioning themselves. You can demonstrate this for yourself through the following exercises.

>First, begin moving across a gentle slope in a traverse. Lean back until you feel pressure against the rear of your boots. Then lean forward until you feel pressure against the front of your boots. Maintain either position long enough and you will find that effort is involved. Now, locate the position between the two positions where there is no effort or strain. There, in the stance found between the two, you are balanced. You will also discover that, in order to stay balanced, your position will constantly change as you ski.

>Next, make a series of wide, round turns on a gentle slope. Repeat the same exercise. Again find the position in which you are balanced with the least amount of effort.

Your body always tells you when you are in balance. Using your natural balancing ability opens the door to experiencing freedom of movement on skis and increases your ability to learn new movements.

The Use of Gravity

During my first two years of skiing, I experienced skis as heavy, hard to turn, and awkward to maneuver. That experience stayed with me for several years even though I refined my skiing.

When I first started teaching in Sun Valley, I was impressed with the European instructors because of their effortless skiing. They seemed to float down the mountain, never wasting energy, and their skis appeared to be natural extensions of their bodies. Whatever it was they were doing, I wanted to know about it. I studied their movements closely. They were using gravity as a primary source of energy, just as a sailor uses the wind to power his boat or as the martial arts expert uses the energy of his opponent to throw him.

I began to experiment with ways to use the pull of gravity in my own skiing. For example, I had always turned skis through the use of vigorous unweighting, which required a lot of energy. I tried unweighting my skis very little and allowed my body to fall down the hill in the direction of the turn. It worked—and it required eighty percent less energy to initiate a turn on skis!

It is impossible to tell you, specifically, how to use the pull of gravity in your skiing, as it must be done in your own creative way. Incorporating this into your own skiing, though, is incredibly rewarding. The following exercises will help you to experience gravity's effect.

THE BASIC ELEMENTS OF SKIING

Stand in the fall line on a gentle slope, holding yourself with your poles. Now, release your poles and allow yourself to slide straight down the hill. Stand upright, relaxed and balanced over your skis. As you increase speed, you will experience a loss of friction under your skis and an increasing momentum in your body. This speed and momentum can be used to make skiing an effortless sport.

Repeat the same exercise on a steeper slope (preferably a short one) with a flat run-out at the bottom. Notice how much faster the speed and momentum appear. Because of this phenomenon, it is actually easier to negotiate skis on steeper slopes.

At an early point in my career, I noticed that effortless skiers rarely skied at slow speeds. I thought at the time that it was easier (and safer) to turn skis at a very slow speed. It just isn't so. It is actually easier to turn skis at faster rather than slower speeds. This does not mean that you have to ski fast to make skis turn easily. It simply means that less effort is required to turn a pair of skis at ten miles per hour than at five miles per hour. Skis no longer feel cumbersome and difficult to maneuver when speed is used to assist your turns. The skis become extensions of your body, feeling natural, light, and easy to turn.

Efficient Movement

When I watched the best racers in the world, they were like supermen to me. They never made a mistake, and their every movement looked perfectly efficient. I later realized that the best skiers still made mistakes, but they were so efficient in their recovery that it was hard to detect "errors."

I wanted to become a very accomplished skier, so I started copying the top skiers. That worked to a degree, but I still didn't *feel* efficient. I realized that I had fallen into the trap of assuming what I thought to be a proper position on skis, rather than letting my *body* dictate the most efficient movement for the situation. I was attempting to perfectly duplicate someone else and disregarding my own experience. It didn't work. What did work was adopting an observed movement and allowing my body to recreate that movement in its own unique way, using my own experience of the situation to guide me.

For example, I was skiing with a friend who continually experienced extreme tiredness in his legs after skiing a moguled run. I asked him to become aware of the point in time when his legs started getting tired. He skied about one hundred yards down a bumpy slope and stopped, feeling strain in his legs. I asked him what he was doing with his upper body while he was skiing.

"I'm imitating the best racers," he said. "They carry their bodies in a low position over the skis."

I asked him how far he thought he could walk without strain if he was constantly bent over. He smiled and said, "Not very far."

He was immediately aware that he was putting himself in a position of constant tension; he realized that he needed to allow himself to stand up and relax while skiing the bumps. Once he saw that efficient movement is created by becoming aware of inefficient movement, he knew exactly what was necessary to improve his approach to skiing moguls.

You, too, should be aware that what is efficient for a racer is not necessarily efficient for a freestyle skier and so on. The goals you have in skiing will act as your guide for creating your own efficient movements. Eliminating inefficiency heightens the sensation of physical freedom unique to skiing. Simple, efficient movement can also eliminate many of those aching muscles and allow you to finish a day of skiing feeling physically refreshed and satisfied with your achievements.

A second, invaluable thing I learned from watching top skiers was that they used an erect posture to carry their weight. Their muscles were free to do the directing and guiding of the skis. In other words, they were using their skeletal structure to bear the weight of their bodies.

I experimented with various "postures" on skis. I found that, when my skeleton was bearing my weight, I could ski long runs nonstop, and arrive at the bottom without breathing hard or experiencing muscle fatigue. Watch any good ski instructor to understand this principle.

The following exercises will help you discover efficient usage of your skeletal structure.

Traverse slowly across a gentle slope and bend forward at the waist. Hold that position while you are moving. Repeat this traverse and lower your body to a seated position over your heels. What are your muscles telling you in these extreme positions?

Traverse a second time on this gentle slope in an upright, relaxed stance. Watch for any effort or strain in your ankles, thighs, back, neck, and arms. Keep adjusting and relaxing any tension until you discover

THE BASIC ELEMENTS OF SKIING

*the stance requiring the least amount of effort. Is
your skeleton bearing your weight?*

Repeat this exercise on a moderately steep slope, again finding the stance that requires the least amount of effort. If you begin to incorporate this exercise into your everyday skiing, you will see that your skeletal structure can bear your weight with very little help from the muscles.

Another thing I noticed about the movements of accomplished skiers was their use of rhythm. They could be racing, mogul skiing, or skiing ice, powder, or crud, but they always skied with rhythm. The rhythm was not always regular. Sometimes it was syncopated, like jazz music (imagine a freestyle skier in moguls); ornate and classical like Bach (imagine a downhill racer); or melodic and graceful (imagine a skier in billowing powder). Without rhythm, a skier appears awkward and expends a great deal of unnecessary energy.

Rhythm is easy to experience. It's innate and natural. Just as the rhythmical beating of your heart or your walking and running rhythms are natural, you have the same ability to ski with natural rhythm. Become aware of the rhythm within yourself and allow it to become a part of your skiing.

Experience the effect of rhythm in the following exercise.

Traverse about sixty feet across a gentle slope, moving at a very slow speed, and perform a tight, quick turn at the far side of the slope. When the turn is complete, traverse another sixty feet, again moving very slowly, and make another tight quick turn. Continue this for another three or four turns with long traverses in between.

Did you notice the sudden energy demand when you made a tight, quick turn from a slow traverse? Did you feel as though you were making efficient use of your energy?

Next, perform a series of continuous turns on the same slope with a short traverse of no more than ten feet between each turn. Let the end of each turn flow easily into the next and develop a natural rhythm with your turns. Do about eight turns in this manner and stop.

Did you see that an easy rhythm required less energy to initiate each of the turns? Did you notice that when your body was moving in rhythm, it was easier to maintain balance?

Employing rhythm in all aspects of your skiing will increase your ability to ski without effort and improve the efficiency of your movements on skis.

Harmonizing with the Terrain

During the first season I skied, I often experienced days when I was out of synchronization with the mountain. It seemed as though I would hit every nasty mogul, every bad patch of ice, and turn across all the wrong ruts. At first, I thought it was just "not my day." Then I saw that accomplished skiers did not seem to have these problems. I began to watch them closely and saw that they were very smart about where they skied. Rather than giving up or beating the mountain to death, they continually looked for ways to move in harmony with the mountain, regardless of the terrain or snow conditions.

If a good skier crossed a patch of ice, he would keep his skis in the fall line and brake his speed on the good snow below the ice. Or, he would simply avoid the ice altogether. If there was a series of nasty ruts, he would ski with the ruts (in the same direction as the ruts) rather than rattle across them. If the moguls were bad, he would choose a path without tough bumps, or ski down the side of the run, avoiding the bad moguls altogether. I have watched Olympic champions do the same thing. Their attitude was, "Why ruin a good run by skiing through some really lousy moguls?" The more I watched good skiers, the more I saw that they were ingenious about the way they worked with the mountain, rather than against it.

You can explore harmonious movement through this next exercise.

Pick an intermediate slope with medium-sized moguls. Find a traverse line with three or four moguls in the path. Traverse across these moguls at slow speed and remain as rigid as possible in the ankles, knees, and hips. You will definitely not experience harmony with the mountain.

Traverse a second time across the same moguls. Allow your skis to contour the terrain like water flowing over rocks. Remain in a tall, relaxed stance between moguls.

Throughout this exercise, do whatever is necessary to keep your weight over your feet. When you cross the crest of each bump, allow your legs to fold up toward your chest, thus absorbing the bump. Extend your legs as you come off the crest of the bump and return to a high, relaxed stance on your skis.

Did you experience moving in harmony with the terrain? This is only one of many ways to move in harmony with the mountain. Very accomplished skiers are constantly creating and discovering new ways to ski with less resistance. After twelve years of professional skiing, I still discover new ways of moving harmoniously with the mountain every time I ski. The process is never ending and always rewarding; it allows me to continue expanding my experience of effortlessness and freedom of movement on skis.

The Anatomy of a Ski

When I first started skiing, I felt that skis were insensitive, awkward, and poorly designed. They felt heavy, clumsy, and definitely not easy to turn. I felt this way until someone showed me the basic design characteristics of a ski. When I saw that skis were actually designed to turn, I was able to employ that knowledge in my everyday skiing. Very soon, I experienced skis as being light, quick, responsive, easy to turn, and natural extensions of my feet.

An understanding of the basic design of all skis will assist you in seeing that they are thoughtfully designed to make your skiing experience an easier one.

The first basic design consideration of a ski is the **side camber** or **side cut.** Side camber is the arc found along the sides of the skis when you place them on the floor, side by side, so they are touching at the tip and tail. This arc causes your ski to turn when you put it on an edge on the snow. It is actually impossible for a ski to travel in a straight line when it is on an edge—*it must turn* because of its side cut.

The second basic design consideration is **bottom camber.** Bottom camber is the arch in the skis observable when they are placed bottom to bottom. This arch distributes your weight from tip to tail while you are skiing and provides a longer platform of stability.

The third basic design consideration of a ski is its **flex pattern** or the manner in which a ski flexes as it is moving over the snow. You can see this pattern by standing the ski in a vertical position with the tail of the ski on the ground, slightly in front of you, with the top facing you. Hold the tip with your left hand and place your right palm against the center of the ski. Pull with your left hand and push with your right hand so you bend the ski. The shape of the curve formed as you push is the flex pattern. The ability of the ski to flex allows the skis to ride over obstacles (such as moguls) and assists the side camber of the ski in creating the round shape of a turn.

There are many other factors in the design of a ski such as swing weight, torsional rigidity, ski length, construction method, materials of construction, etc. These factors all contribute to the design of skis for different purposes. Downhill skis are totally different from free-style skis, as slalom skis are totally different from recreational short skis.

In the beginning, though, the most valuable thing for you to realize is that a ski is designed to turn. If you simply ride the edges of the skis, *they will turn by themselves.* It is also valuable to know that skis are designed for specific purposes. Choosing a slalom ski is unwise if you desire to be a recreational skier. Pick skis that are designed for your needs.

The Basic Elements of a Turn

The first four years I skied, I did not understand the mechanics of a turn. I thought it was some complicated maneuver requiring discipline and skill to learn. When I realized how simple it was to perform a turn, the whole sport of skiing became incredibly simple and uncomplicated. A turn is nothing more than changing edges. When I knew that, I could create turns that were comfortable and effective for me.

The purpose of a turn is to change the direction of movement and to create resistance against the snow, thereby controlling speed.

A turn consists of two parts—the initiation and the completion. That is all. The initiation, during which the edges are changed, happens when the resistance you have created against the snow is momentarily broken through unweighting, stemming, stepping, etc. The particular form of the initiation does not matter. What *is* important is changing the edges of the skis in order to change direction.

The second part of a turn is the completion—the major portion of any turn and also the easiest. In this part of the turn, you ride on the edges of the skis until the skis have turned across the hill and your speed has been reduced to a point at which you can initiate another turn. It is valuable to recognize that the completion of one turn is also the beginning of the next. Knowing this helps to incorporate rhythm into your skiing and to experience the simplicity of a series of linked turns.

Controlling Your Speed

Even after two years of teaching beginning and intermediate skiers, I had trouble controlling my speed on skis. On steep slopes, I would accelerate with each turn; on medium slopes at fast speeds, my skis felt unpredictable and were prone to wandering. When I watched good skiers, I saw that they always had their speed under control and that their skis moved with certainty over the snow.

As I continued watching good skiers, I realized that they were constantly creating resistance between their skis and the snow, and that was *the key to controlling speed.* I incorporated their movements into my own skiing, thus discovering an ability to control speed on skis that had always seemed impossible. If you want to control speed on skis, develop your ability to create resistance between your skis and the snow.

Resistance is created through various kinds of turns, the simplest form being a **skidded turn.** We all use this turn when we are first learning to ski. Skidding the skis through a turn offers little resistance to the snow; it works well on very gentle slopes and at slow speeds. During a skidded turn, the skis are almost flat on the snow. This kind of turn is also used by experts at moments when it is unwise to use too much edge. An example of a series of skidded turns is found on pages 98-99 in the sequence entitled "Wide-Track Turn."

The second form of a turn is a skidded turn with a **check,** or a sudden edging of the skis that creates a fast braking action of a skier's momentum. A check is a dramatic, short-lived increase of resistance between the skis and the snow. It can be used during various parts of the turn. It is most frequently used at the bottom of a turn to brake speed and initiate the next turn. An example of turns with checks can be seen on pages 102-103 in the sequence entitled "Unweighted Parallel Turn." The check is the moment in the turn before unweighting. Observe the braking action of the skis and their increasing resistance against the snow.

The third form of creating resistance is through **carving.** Carving is nothing more than minimizing the amount of skid during the turn. When a turn is carved, the skis appear to cut the snow, hence the name. A carved turn creates the most prolonged resistance between the skis and the snow and is the single most effective means of controlling speed during a turn. It can be accomplished by using the entire length of the ski—the tip, the tail, or various parts of the ski—during the time a turn takes place. A carved turn leaves a definite, narrow track that is round and uniform in its shape. Carved turns are used by all accomplished skiers to gain maximum control under all snow and slope conditions. Many of the sequences later in the book illustrate various forms of carved turns.

A way to increase the effectiveness of a carved turn is through **early edging,** or more specifically through the application of edge and pressure on the skis before they enter the fall line. Early edging can be executed in any type of turn; even a simple stem christie can be edged early and carved throughout the duration of the turn. Accomplished skiers use early edging to control their speed as they enter each turn. This has the effect of reducing their speed before they reach the fall line (when the skis are pointed straight down the hill), thereby increasing their ability to control their speed at the bottom of the turn. Developing early edging is a necessity for accomplished, controlled skiing on steeper slopes. Refer to the sequence titled "Early Edging" on page 113 for a specific illustration of two carved turns. Study the tracks and note the narrow track left by the carving skis.

A further aspect of creating resistance in turns is through the **shape of the turn** itself. Every carved turn inscribes an arc on the snow; the shape of this arc and its relationship to the fall line can have a significant bearing on increasing or decreasing the speed of a skier as he executes a turn. Accomplished skiers consciously create turns that are very round in order to gain maximum resistance and control with each turn. Accomplished skiers can create round turns regardless of slope or snow conditions.

Another significant factor in creating resistance with each turn is the amount and nature of ski-to-snow contact during a turn. If a ski is in contact with the snow throughout the turn, there is more resistance and more control. If there is down pressure on the ski during the radius of the turn, there is even more effective ski-to-snow contact. Reducing this down pressure causes the skis to accelerate through the turn. Racers use this to their advantage. The French call it *glissement,* the ability to maintain the direction and control of a turn without over-edging or putting unnecessary pressure on the skis in the turn, just enough to keep the turn going without slowing the skis. An example of poor ski-to-snow contact is the skier who edges his skis at the top of the turn without putting pressure on them. Even though the skis are edged, he will accelerate as he comes out of the turn in an uncontrollable manner.

Creating Stability on Skis

Until late in my skiing career, I assumed that it was necessary to change my body position on skis each time I encountered a different slope or snow condition. When I watched the best skiers in the world, though, I saw that they did not change their basic stance on skis regardless of where or what they were skiing. My subsequent experiments proved that it was unnecessary to change my stance on skis every time I met with adverse snow and slope conditions. I discovered that there are two simple principles which allow the skier to become very stable under all snow and slope conditions.

1. **Keep your torso quiet.** Keeping your weight constantly over your feet enables your legs to steer the skis with a high degree of control. A quiet upper body also allows you to work with your hands and poles in the most effective manner possible.

2. Keep your torso perpendicular to the slope. Following this rule keeps your body weight constantly over your skis, regardless of the steepness of the slope.

When you follow these two principles under all skiing conditions, you will increase your ability to stay on balance, very rarely lose your balance, increase the efficient use of the skis, ski with less effort, and regain your balance easily and quickly when you do lose it.

The Function of Equipment

I used to think that it was necessary to have the latest gear to become an accomplished skier. Good equipment is a help, but only as long as it suits your purpose. When I had the opportunity to ski with some of the best skiers in the world, I saw that they used only the equipment that adapted to their needs in skiing. When I began to choose equipment based on the following principles, my skiing improved.

Skis should be of design characteristics that comply with your purpose in skiing. Do not choose slalom skis if you want to ski powder. Skis should be of high enough quality to give you *at least* two seasons of skiing even if you ski every day. Choose skis that are of an appropriate length for your ability and needs.

Boots are designed to protect your feet from the snow, give your ankles support, and increase your ability to maneuver the skis. They should first of all be comfortable and fit well. If they do not, don't buy them. They should give your ankles adequate lateral stability for your purposes and aid in your ability to maneuver the skis. If you are a recreational skier, do not choose boots that are designed for slalom racing; choose boots that will suit your purpose.

Bindings are designed to attach the skis firmly to your feet and provide a safety factor in case of a fall. Choose bindings that are of high quality and keep them clean and well maintained. Choose an appropriate design and spring loading for your purposes. And, again, be certain that your bindings and boots are compatible in design. For example, if you are a recreational skier, do not purchase bindings that are intended for racing.

Poles are designed to assist your balance as you ski. If you want to know how important they are, try skiing without them for a few runs. They should be of sufficient quality to avoid accidental breakage (in the shaft, basket, or grip) and be of a length appropriate for your height and skiing requirements. Poles that are either too long or too short are a detriment to balance while skiing.

Following these guidelines will enable you to avoid the pitfall of choosing equipment that is not designed for your purposes. For example, if you are a recreational skier who likes to ski moguls, it would be very unwise to purchase skis, boots, and bindings that were designed specifically for slalom racing. Slalom racing equipment can detract from the fun of skiing under most recreational skiing conditions.

I've observed that the nine Elements of Skiing presented in this chapter are the foundation of all technical systems of skiing. I am not presenting these Elements as ultimate truths about skiing, but simply as the primary guiding elements in the careers of many successful skiers. Employing these Elements in my own skiing has given me a solid base for expanding my abilities and becoming an accomplished skier. They have been presented for you to employ in your own skiing. And, as with all the material in this book, do not take any of it at face value. Try these things out for yourself, and if they work within your experience of skiing, continue to use them. What is most important is that you find the basic elements in skiing that work best for you.

5

Becoming an Accomplished Skier

Anyone can become an accomplished skier. An accomplished skier can be defined as someone capable of skiing anywhere, at any time, under any conditions. No slope, weather, or snow condition is too difficult for the accomplished skier to handle.

Boarding an aerial tramway somewhere in the world, rising 9,000 vertical feet, finding yourself in the midst of some of the oldest and most spectacular mountains on earth is an incredible experience. The scenery is so astounding that it creates a feeling of unreality. And what an incredible sensation it is to stand on a stunning white ridge of snow outlined against a brilliant blue sky and know that you can jump off that ridge, leave the earth, and experience flight.

It is impossible to communicate the experience of skiing at forty miles per hour on open fields of summer snow at an altitude of 12,000 feet, seeing green valleys, glowing like emeralds in the summer sun, laid out at your feet. It is even more impossible to describe the thrill of approaching a man-made jump, knowing that you are going to put your body into a somersaulting flight. Time stops for a moment and you become a bird, free from gravity and able to see the world from a point of view that few human beings ever experience.

The sensation of being dropped at the top of a mountain by jet helicopter into the middle of a winter wilderness is impossible to imagine. When the helicopter leaves, you experience a sense of quiet and oneness with nature unique to mountains in winter. As you descend through this white wilderness, the powder snow billows seventy feet behind you and hangs sparkling on the deep blue horizon. You know you are the master.

These descriptions are only an inkling of the vast scope of the experiences shared by accomplished skiers. These kinds of experiences are open to anyone who wants to achieve them.

During the time I have been a professional skier, I have noticed a similarity of attitudes among the most successful skiers and athletes in any sport. If you desire to be an accomplished skier, then knowing these attitudes will be of value to you.

I had an opportunity to talk with Jean-Claude Killy one evening at his home in Val D'Isere, France. I asked him how he was able to retire from skiing for one full year (after winning three gold medals at the Grenoble Olympics) and then, upon his return to professional skiing, win the World Professional Championships in his first season of competition. Bear in mind that professional ski racing is totally different from amateur racing and requires a whole new attitude and set of skills.

He thought for a moment and replied, "If you're going to do something, you might as well do it first class." He could not envision putting his energy into achieving a goal without doing it totally. For him, the commitment to pro racing was one hundred percent, no less.

He also stated something by omission. He had no reason to believe that he could not achieve his goal. This same attitude is prevalent among all successful skiers, including myself: **"There is no reason I can't do it."**

Here is another example of this attitude from a two-time European Rallye Racing Champion named Jean. Rallye Racing is auto racing on mountain roads; it involves a driver, a navigator, high-powered cars, precise timing, and a lot of skill. Jean gave me a lesson on ice driving at Isola 2000, a ski resort in the Maritime Alps of southern France.

One particular turn on the course was shaped like a hairpin; it was icy and difficult to get through. Jean was teaching me to enter this turn at full speed (fifty miles per hour on pure ice) by throwing the car completely sideways and pulling on the hand brake. On each circuit of the course, I was so scared that I gave up in the middle of the hairpin turn and landed the car squarely in the snowbank. On my fourth try, as we were sliding toward the snowbank out of control, Jean lost his temper and yelled in my ear: "You're giving up! You must never give up! You must never stop believing that the car is going to make it through the turn!"

I really heard what he said. I decided to try it one more time, no matter how scared I became. It worked. I managed to get the car through the turn and keep it on the road. I felt elated! Perhaps it wasn't the most beautiful execution of that turn, but it did not matter. I knew I could do it. What had worked was simply to believe, with no doubt, that somehow the car would get through the turn.

Jean later explained that he had learned early in his driving career that this attitude could help him win races. He also added that this same attitude had saved his life on two occasions when his car seemed totally out of control. I have recognized for some time that this attitude (call it single-mindedness) is the single most important factor in the careers of all successful skiers.

The information presented in this chapter is taken from personal experiences of many, very accomplished skiers. If you know there is no reason you cannot achieve what you want in skiing, then this chapter will be of particular value to you in pursuing your goal of becoming an accomplished skier.

Set Your Goal

When I was fourteen, I set very clear goals about what I wanted to achieve in skiing and committed myself to achieving those goals. Keeping those goals in mind has kept me on the track, and I've seen the same kind of goal-setting work for many others. I didn't know it at the time, but by establishing my goals, I had taken the first step toward realizing what I wanted in skiing.

When you know your goal, it is then helpful to examine any negative beliefs you may have about achieving that goal. Incredible barriers can be created by your beliefs. Your reasons may sound perfectly logical: "I don't have enough time to ski"; "I'm too old to learn to ski well"; "It takes too many years to get there"; or "I was raised in the city and I don't have an aptitude for the outdoors."

These simple, logical reasons can keep you from achieving what you desire in skiing. Become aware of these negative beliefs, and then create opposite positive beliefs that are in line with your goal. In this way, you can effectively move in the direction of achieving your goal. Also be aware of the negative beliefs held by the people around you; they can have a strong influence should you choose to believe them.

When I first started learning somersaults on skis, there were many people who thought it was a crazy idea and that it could never be done safely. I chose to listen to the people who said, "If you really want to do it, it can be done." It was valuable to continually seek out the people whose ideas and beliefs supported me in the attainment of my personal goals.

Goal-setting works for all of us, regardless of how far we want to go in skiing or how much we want to achieve. For example, if you are going on a one-week ski vacation, set a goal for yourself that you can achieve or come close to achieving by the end of the week. It might be simple, like being able to ski a particular run, nonstop, by the end of week, or being able to ski with a more advanced skier. In this way, you can measure your achievements of the week and finish your vacation with a sense of accomplishment, knowing that you have measurably improved your skiing.

Be Willing

If you want to achieve your goal in skiing, you need to do whatever is necessary to achieve your goal. You must be willing to handle any and all things that stand in the way of achieving your goal, including giving up other things and experiencing discomfort and frustration from time to time.

One of the first ski teaching jobs I held was in a ski area where rain was a fairly common occurrence during the ski season. I remember standing out in the rain, feeling the water drip off my nose and fill my boots. A cold wind was driving sleet into the faces of the skiers in my class. I wondered, "What am I doing here?" Then I reminded myself of my goal—"I'm learning everything I can about skiing, and it's necessary for me to be here." I stayed and continued working toward my goal.

Sometimes you can reach a point at which you feel like giving up, and it seems as though it isn't worth the struggle any more. These are the times when you need to be willing to review your situation and feelings. Is your goal worth achieving? If it is, then what are these emotions and feelings? Are they ideas and beliefs that are barriers to achieving what you want? Reviewing these beliefs at a time when you feel like giving up is extremely valuable. It gives you a chance to see if you still want to accomplish your goal; and if you do, you will begin to see what is in your way.

A willingness to constantly review and consider what barriers are in the way of achieving goals is a characteristic of many successful skiers. When you really want to achieve something, you must be willing to be afraid, get embarrassed, make mistakes, fail, succeed, lose, win, get uncomfortable, etc. The more willing you are to do whatever is necessary to achieve your goal, the easier the goal becomes to achieve. The only thing that ever holds anyone back from becoming a very accomplished skier is his lack of willingness to do whatever is necessary to achieve the level he desires.

Your Self-Confidence

Self-confidence is having that innate, complete trust in yourself. No matter what happens, you can achieve what you want. When you are confident about yourself and your abilities, you will recognize that, when you have a bad day, it doesn't mean anything. You just had a bad day. When you trust yourself, you don't berate yourself for doing poorly. You accept it and say, "That didn't work too well." You keep moving forward, knowing your performance will improve.

The foundation of your self-confidence can be built from consciously recognizing all the things you have achieved in the past. It may seem silly to acknowledge your ability to put your skis on well, but that is where self-confidence starts, by recognizing the simple things you can do. Start focusing your attention on and building upon the experience of the things you do well.

For example, when I was first learning to ski, I had set a goal of skiing the challenging run underneath the chairlift. One day the opportunity came. I bought a chairlift ticket, stapled it to my parka and was immediately terrified! I had to do it. I was committed. Doubts raced through my mind like crazy. I didn't trust myself, and my self-confidence was rapidly vanishing.

Then I thought: "Wait a minute! I don't need to scare myself like this. I know I can ski that run, and I don't care what I look like coming down. I'm even willing to crawl down the steep places if I have to." I decided to trust myself.

I rode the lift to the top, skied the hill (with no need to crawl down any part of it) and felt terrific! I trusted myself and it worked. The rest of that day was spent skiing that run and having a great time.

The point of the story is that I set a goal of skiing a challenging run. When I committed myself to doing it, I experienced self-doubt and dwindling self-confidence. When I recognized self-doubt, I (immediately) reminded myself of what I could already do and looked at all of the ways to accomplish my goal, including being willing to crawl down the steep stuff. In doing that, I re-established my self-confidence to accomplish what I wanted.

If you experience a situation where you lack self-confidence, using this process can help you continue toward your goal. For example, imagine yourself standing at the top of an intimidating slope. As you look at this slope, envision another similar slope that you skied with confidence. Recall your ability to operate in other challenging circumstances. Begin to imagine what you could do on the areas of this slope that seem difficult. Now, when you've imagined how you can ski the different parts of that slope under control, imagine yourself skiing the entire run using the ways created in your imagination.

Using this process of looking to your past accomplishments and moments of self-confidence, you can build and increase your confidence in pursuing present goals.

Your Physical Condition

Physical conditioning is a process of putting your body into a condition in which it can function well in skiing. I used to feel that to be in "good physical condition," it was necessary to train vigorously for many months, and then ski for two or three weeks, before I could begin to enjoy and to improve upon my abilities. I actually felt guilty when I started a season knowing that I hadn't been following a rigid training schedule. I felt frustrated because I believed I should be training and I wasn't.

Then I realized that my skiing was improving each year even though I wasn't "doing what I thought I should" to be in good physical shape. I started looking around and noticed some interesting things about people and their attempts to get in shape. I saw that for many people, it was difficult to maintain a steady schedule of exercise. They also expended a lot of mental and physical energy trying to get in shape for skiing and were not meeting with a great deal of success. Frequently they dropped out of their programs in frustration. Not only were people unsuccessful at getting in shape, they had no fun in the process. What I am trying to point out is that many people meet with a great deal of frustration trying to get in shape and perhaps there is a way to enjoy physical conditioning through a different approach.

Last season I did a three-month promotional tour that involved excessive sitting, standing, eating, etc. This tour was not what most people would recommend for "getting in shape for skiing." At the end of the tour I returned to Snowbird. I took my first run of the year with a friend who had been following a fairly rigid schedule of physical exercise during the fall. He was also a very good skier. We started from the top together, and I arrived at the bottom feeling great. I felt almost no exhaustion or lack of wind. My friend arrived winded and fighting a case of burning thighs. We discussed this seemingly strange situation on the way up the lift.

What struck us both was that it is not necessary to be in top physical condition to ski with a high degree of skill. Furthermore, being in top physical condition does not necessarily guarantee one effortless skiing.

He asked me my feelings about skiing a first run of the season, and I told him that I knew that I could ski down any slope, at any time, regardless of how much physical conditioning I had done. I also mentioned that to me skiing was more a matter of efficient movement than of physical conditioning. I've always felt that skiing was far less energy-consuming than running or playing football. At the same time, I knew if I wanted to ski long fast runs, or long runs through moguls, more skiing was necessary to gradually build my endurance and strength.

My friend recognized that he held very strong beliefs about the need to condition himself for sports. First, he believed that he couldn't ski his best if he was not in top physical condition. He believed that, in order to ski moguls well, he had to be in super physical condition in order to maintain a low position over his skis. He further discovered that he believed he could not ski well for the first two or three weeks of the season, regardless of his physical condition.

We both realized that physical conditioning is certainly worthwhile, but it alone will not create the skier. The beliefs we have about needing to be in shape will have a far greater effect on our performance.

During the fourteen years that I have been a professional skier, I have never followed a rigid discipline of any type. Certainly it is necessary to be in good, strong physical condition to ski at the peak of one's ability, as in the case of a professional racer or downhill racer. All I am saying is that it is not necessary to maintain a rigid training schedule in order to experience ourselves as accomplished skiers. It is only necessary to be in a physical condition that is appropriate for the level at which you wish to participate in skiing. If you attempt to perform too far beyond the level of your current physical state, your body will let you know it—aching muscles, tiredness, etc. Increasing your capacity for improved physical performance is best done in small steps (run a quarter mile, then one mile, then one and a quarter, etc.) so that you don't strain your physical system. Increasing your capacity for performance can also be a great deal of fun.

What has worked well for me has been a program of relatively constant physical activity. Rather than going out and doing regularly scheduled exercise, I simply do the physical things I love to do when I feel like doing them. I have a trampoline in my back yard. When I feel like improving my acrobatics or taking a break from office work, I'll jump on the trampoline for a couple of hours. Sometimes I'll feel like playing tennis. I'll call a friend and go do that. Three or four times a year I'll take a two-day hike into the mountains. I do these things with the intention of getting exercise, having fun, and staying active.

Examine your beliefs about physical conditioning using the processes discussed earlier in this book. Become clear about what kind and what amount of physical conditioning you need to best suit your desired level of performance in skiing. Remember, you don't have to train like a professional football player to be a good recreational skier. Create an activity schedule that you enjoy. Have fun and alter your physical condition in the process.

Create Your Challenge

One of the real joys in skiing is setting a challenge for yourself and then completing that challenge. It is a primary key in the expansion of your abilities. I've skied for eighteen years and still find new challenges each day.

Pick challenges that are constructive and will assist you in reaching your goal. Each day you ski, you can find a new challenge. It doesn't have to be difficult; rather, it should be something that is achievable. That way, you get to win and feel good each day that you ski.

For example, when I was a ski instructor, I decided I wanted to be able to ski in all kinds of snow. There was a spot on the mountain where I taught that always had wind-blown, junk snow. I started by setting a simple challenge. First I wanted to be able to traverse in that stuff. Every lunch hour I'd go to that spot full of junk snow and practice just traversing through it. I got to the point at which I could move through that junk with real confidence.

Then I set a new challenge: Make one turn and stand up. After a few days I could make one turn and stand up. I followed this process of creating new challenges every few days, and before long, I was able to ski junk snow very well. The key was in picking the challenges that continued developing my ability to ski junk snow and were easy enough for me to achieve.

The following is a list of challenges that has worked for many skiers. These are the kinds of challenges that accomplished skiers create for themselves every day they ski. It is necessary to give yourself specific challenges at which you know you can succeed. That way, you can smile at the end of the day and compliment yourself on your achievement. Use your imagination and have fun with the challenges that you use from this list and with the ones you create from your own imagination.

- Ski a trail or slope that you wouldn't ordinarily ski.
- Traverse a moguled slope at high speed.
- Ski long runs nonstop.
- Ski a run making nothing but long, round turns.
- Ski a moguled slope staying in the fall line, and maintain a constant rate of speed. Increase your speed with each run.
- Ski crud snow conditions. Don't avoid those nasty patches of crummy snow.
- Practice running slalom gates.
- Practice running giant slalom gates.
- Practice round, wide turns on a medium steep slope.
- Do the same on a steeper slope.
- Do the same as the two exercises above and lift the inside ski with each turn.

- Ski underneath a chairlift. Focus your attention on what you are doing with each turn. Totally forget about the people riding overhead.
- Ski steep chutes using short radius turns.
- Ski steep chutes using long radius turns.
- Ski directly behind someone in the moguls. Duplicate each turn they make. Repeat and increase the speed.
- Ski flat light conditions. Vary the speed and radius of your turns with each run.
- Ski powder at a very slow speed, completing each turn.
- Ski powder at a very high speed, carving round, narrow, uniform turns.
- Drop off small rocks, ledges, etc., in powder snow.
- Find the best skiers on the hill and ski with them.

Observation

Observation is one of the most valuable learning tools we have. It is simply the act of looking at something without evaluation or judgment. In skiing, when you observe, you will see clearly whether something is workable or not.

BECOMING AN ACCOMPLISHED SKIER

It is very easy to fall into the trap of listening to someone, especially a recognized expert, and take what he or she says as the truth. Recognize that what that person is saying works for him—that does not mean it will always work for someone else. Don't disregard what the experts are saying. They offer very valuable information. Simply listen to and observe all sources of information, then try them out in your own skiing.

The judging and evaluating process often clouds our observations and sends us down paths that result in confusion. Here is an example of what I mean.

I knew a fellow a few years ago who wanted to be a very accomplished mogul skier. One day he was watching a group of racers ski a bumpy race course; he noticed that the racers held their hands low and maintained a low body position over their skis *(that is observation)*. He assumed that because racers were good skiers on a bumpy course, the same approach should work while skiing moguls *(that is evaluation and judgment)*. He then tried skiing the bumps with a low body position, holding his hands low like the racers. He met with frustration because what worked on a race course did not necessarily apply to normal bump skiing. He compounded his problem by deciding that he was a crummy skier because he wasn't getting any better at skiing the bumps *(more evaluation and judgment)*. His approach did not work because he assumed that what worked in a bumpy race course would also work in moguls. Had he exercised pure observation about skiing bumps, he would have simply watched what good skiers were doing while skiing normal bumps instead of watching racers ski a course. Out of his observation and personal experience, he would then have discovered what works for him while skiing moguls.

Very successful skiers observe and borrow from all sources to improve their skiing: books, photographs, other skiers, technical systems, films, etc. Any source where they might find something different that allows them to expand their current abilities is considered valuable. They employ observation to see if it works for them. If it does, they keep it; if it doesn't, they throw it out.

The single most valuable source to observe for improving your skiing is another skier. Observe someone doing something on skis that you would like to learn. Let's say you would like to ski powder well. Ask them to demonstrate what they are doing that makes them such good powder skiers. If you can't ski with them, watch them. Study their movements on the hill. Notice what elements make them good powder skiers. You might notice something that a certain skier does with his hands that assists his balance with each turn. Study that movement and then try it for yourself. See if it works for you. Allow for the fact that you will probably not look exactly like the skier from whom you borrowed the movement. You are not the same person. You will, however, create your own version of the same movement.

Observation is the key to finding out what does work, as well as what doesn't work. Our ability to observe is always available to us. Try observing without any evaluation or judgment and see how simple and easy it is to understand the sport of skiing.

Skiing in Your Mind

When I was a teenager, I spent many hours each day dreaming about skiing, especially in study hall. I didn't get much studying done, but I spent a lot of time imagining myself skiing. Though unaware of it at that time, I was using a valid process for improving my skiing without actually going out on the hill.

This mental imagery can be employed through pure imagination or with the use of visual aids (as found in the Visualization chapter later in this book). The following exercise will assist you in the conscious use of your mental skiing ability.

Take a moment, while you are waiting for the bus or riding a chairlift, and choose an aspect of your skiing that needs improvement, your pole plants for example. Now imagine a good skier using his poles. When you visualize that clearly, imagine your-self skiing, using poles in the same manner as the good skier you just pictured.

Take three or four minutes each day and imagine yourself skiing an entire run using this new move-ment. Continue the process without putting a time limit on yourself, such as, "I have to do this turn in two weeks or else."

If you continue to use this process, an alteration will start to take place in your skiing, often in a very short period of time.

I travel frequently and spend many hours on airplanes. In my mind, however, I am bouncing on a trampoline or practicing skiing. Through the use of mental images, I find that I don't have to spend as much time practicing physically. I can go out and do what I've practiced in my mind, and somehow my skiing and my trampoline work have im-proved. The value of this process is particularly noticeable when I am physically inactive over a long period of time and then return to ac-tivity.

Using your imagination allows you to learn faster and increases the fun you have when you are skiing.

Be Attentive

Paying attention to what you are doing develops the ability to "be here now," that is, concentrating your attention totally on what you are doing at the moment. The results of concentrated, total attention are: (1) you enjoy what you are doing; (2) your rate of learning increases (as your mental confusion diminishes); and (3) it is possible to enter an extraordinary state of mind. It's a state in which time seems suspended. The mind becomes quiet and the body moves from a condition of constant reaction to the incredibly effective state of pure action. You may be physically traveling at high speed, but your conscious awareness is *experiencing* all movement in slow motion.

Examples of this suspended time state are quoted frequently by Formula I racing drivers. They drive under competitive conditions at speeds of up to 200 miles per hour. It is impossible for their minds to operate effectively at these speeds. It is necessary for these drivers to move out of their minds and into this state of "no-mind" as they accelerate to racing speeds. All of these drivers have developed the ability to enter this no-mind state for extended periods of time. They describe this state as one of "slow-motion"; even at speeds of 200 miles per hour they have very little sensation of speed.

Mental interruptions in skiing can be just as detrimental to the performance of a skier as they can to the performance of a racing driver.

These interruptions come about when we are worried about doing well, winning the race, concerned about being embarrassed in front of people, etc. These distractions cause us to become momentarily lost in the dialogue of our minds.

I can illustrate this with a recent experience I had when I was part of an acrobatic jumping team. We were demonstrating aerial acrobatics on an artificial ski jump. It was my turn in the progression of the show to perform a back layout somersault. I was standing at the top of the jump when suddenly I couldn't pay attention to what I was doing. I became involved in a mental dialogue: "If I blow this jump, the people (2000 of them) out there are going to be disappointed and think I'm not as good as I'm supposed to be. I didn't practice this jump enough before the show. What am I doing on this crazy, high platform anyway?" All of this dialogue took me completely out of the experience of jumping.

I found a very effective way of breaking the dialogue and returning to what I was doing. I reminded myself of my purpose in being where I was at the moment. In the middle of this mental chatter I said, "Wait a minute! What am I supposed to do now? I am supposed to do a back layout somersault. Do I know how to do a back layout somersault? Yes. Well, am I ready to do it? Yes." I pushed off and performed the jump. I recognized that, when the dialogue stopped, I restored my self-confidence and was able to focus my attention on my jumping.

All top skiers and athletes have developed the ability to stop these mental interruptions and focus totally on the task at hand. Focusing your attention on what you are doing at the moment is a major key in allowing your body to perform at maximum efficiency. It is in this state that athletes turn in their best performances and achieve the impossible.

Handling Your Fear

Fear is when you experience anxiety about real or imagined danger. You can recognize the signs of fear through your body; "butterflies in the stomach," "cotton mouth," trembling, etc. It is necessary to handle your fear if you wish to become an accomplished skier. This process is actually very simple.

When I first started skiing, everyone told me that skiing was dangerous and that people playing football or baseball should not ski because they might break a leg. I assumed that skiing must be dangerous, though I still wanted to ski. During my third week on skis, I heard that a girl, supposedly an accomplished skier, had broken her leg on a steep slope. This immediately reinforced my idea: skiing was dangerous, particularly on steep slopes.

When I went to Sun Valley to teach skiing, I saw a number of accomplished skiers skiing and enjoying steep slopes. Why weren't they afraid? Were steep slopes harmless after all? I began to question my beliefs about the danger of skiing steep slopes, and I saw that most of my ideas came from what other people had told me. I also saw that I had spent many years focusing on the danger of steep slopes and had produced a lot of fear (bodily reactions) in myself. The steep slopes were not causing me to be afraid. The ideas I had accumulated and believed were the source of my fear.

I decided that the best way to overcome my fear was to ski short, steep slopes. After a few runs, my fear began to diminish and I felt more confident. I thought, "Now I'll try one a little steeper and a little longer." I did, and again my fear diminished. As I continued this process, my fear gradually disappeared and I found new confidence in myself. Steep slopes stopped looking so steep and actually looked easy to ski. I began to enjoy skiing them.

Look within your own experience of skiing, and see if you haven't made fear disappear. It might be a simple example, like the way you felt the first time you put on skis. Do you still feel that way, or has your fear gone away?

Fear can be an ally, an early warning system that tells you that you are approaching your limit. It is valuable because it tells you to go easy in order to accomplish what you are doing with safety. Sometimes you can see that you are "in over your head." When you realize this, perhaps the wisest decision is to back off and wait until another time. When fear functions as an early warning system, it is up to you to pay heed and make your own choice about continuing or waiting until another day. When you are concerned about your personal safety, you will always make the right choice.

Becoming the master of your fear is a never-ending process in becoming an accomplished skier. Handling fear is a necessary step in reaching your goals. You can experience a great sense of pride when you recognize that you have set a challenge, handled your fear, and accomplished what you set out to do.

Creating Personal Safety

Personal safety comes from a sense of trust in yourself, a trust that you don't have to injure yourself, knowing that you can always avoid dangerous situations. A loss of that trust comes through an accumulation of negative beliefs. For example, if you hold an attitude like, "I don't stand a chance out there because of all the other crazy skiers," or "I know my time is up this year and I'm due for an accident," then you are directing your energy toward accidents rather than away from them. You may not actually have an accident, but you are allowing your mental energy to run in that direction.

It's just as easy to build beliefs that run in the opposite direction. For example: "I know that I can walk up and down stairs safely, so there is no reason I can't ski safely." "I have no desire to get hurt, so if I see a dangerous situation I will simply avoid it." Or, "If my friends ask me to do something I don't feel safe doing, I'll politely refuse." This isn't to say that you should make excuses for yourself. I am saying that focusing your attention in the direction of not having accidents, as well as creating beliefs that support your personal safety, is a primary factor in avoiding injury.

I used to hold the point of view that accidents just happen, that is, until I started reviewing my personal experience of accidents. Earlier in my skiing career I had two serious injuries. I believed that the cause of my accidents was that my skis were too long, the snow was bad, my bindings didn't work properly, I was too tired, etc. Certainly all of these things contributed to my injuries.

I recently reviewed my state of mind at the time of the accidents, and I saw some surprising things. The accidents I had were not so accidental. I discovered that immediately preceding the accidents I was very upset and my state of mind was angry and clouded. That emotional situation had existed with me for several months. I recalled that, during this confusing and unstable time, I had actually considered breaking a leg as a solution to my problems! Personal confusion and dissatisfaction added to my chances of experiencing an injury.

Now I have no reason or desire to have an accident—I would gain nothing. I avoid putting myself in situations in which I could experience an accident, and I continue to operate in the areas in which I know I can always handle myself. If I'm not feeling confident, or if I'm experiencing fear to the point at which it's controlling my body, I simply don't do what looks dangerous. I do what I know I can accomplish without injury. When my fear is gone, I return to the challenge.

There is no reason in the world for you to get hurt skiing. Beware of the desires to please your friends (desires that are stronger than your sense of personal safety) or the desire to vent your personal frustrations while skiing. You can set yourself up to be injured. Regardless of your age, you are capable of operating with total personal safety. When you become aware of your beliefs and feelings about the danger of skiing and focus on new positive thoughts, you can begin to alter those feelings. You have the ability to make skiing a safer experience for yourself, regardless of how far you wish to take your skiing abilities.

Expectations

A trap for all accomplished skiers is the expectation that one must always perform well. This kind of expectation can definitely take the fun out of skiing. There's nothing wrong with performing well; it's an incredible experience. The problem lies in expecting yourself or thinking that others expect you to perform flawlessly at all times. When you have this expectation and don't live up to it, you can feel crushed, defeated. A vicious cycle begins when you start relating your "defeats" to your sense of self-worth. You begin to feel less worthy.

Last fall I had completed two months of travel and was spending my first morning on skis at Snowbird. I was a third of the way down the mountain, complimenting myself on what a good skier I was, and admiring myself for skiing so well on my first day, when a ski patrolman went by me at about twice the speed I was skiing. (I ski very fast.) I immediately found myself in an inner dialogue about how humiliating it was to have a ski patrolman skiing faster and better than myself. "It would take me months of skiing to reach that same level of skiing," I thought to myself. I decided that I should quit skiing and go down to the office and make some phone calls; that way I wouldn't have to be humiliated by ski patrolmen skiing faster and better than myself. The expectation of how well I thought I should be skiing, and the feeling that I wasn't living up to that expectation, totally ruined my day of skiing.

When you have firm expectations about winning a race or performing flawlessly and don't allow for the possibility of losing or making mistakes, you can set yourself up to experience strong disappointment with yourself. An interesting experience often takes place when you are able to drop your expectations and simply perform. A friend of mine who was a two-time Olympic medal winner recently told me this story, which demonstrates what can happen when you have dropped your expectations.

The night before he was to compete in an Olympic slalom event, his coach told him that he could not allow him to compete the next day. My friend was considered a heavy favorite to win the event, and he had spent many years preparing himself for this very race. He was so disappointed that he spent a sleepless night and was prepared to leave the Olympic games the next morning. During breakfast, his coach suddenly reversed his decision and told him he could ski in the event.

He went out on the hill feeling empty. He really didn't care if he won the race or not. He decided to simply do his best, win or lose. In this state, he skied his first run in the slalom and placed two full seconds ahead of the entire field! He'd never skied that well in his life!

As he climbed back up the course, he realized that he actually had an opportunity to win this race and take home a gold medal. The expectations started creeping back. During his second run, he was very cautious and placed ninth. His combined time, though, easily won him a gold medal.

It was a valuable lesson for him. He saw how dramatically his performance improved when he dropped his expectations about winning and turned his attention *totally* to his performance.

When you can go out on the hill without expectations of how good you should be, and can allow yourself to look awkward at times, you can experience your best performance.

Be Aggressive

Aggressiveness is a state of being in which you step out of your mind and operate on a totally physical level. In this state, there is no thinking, only action. When your body operates without interference from the mind, you will find yourself capable of a level of performance that you may not have thought possible. It is impossible to become an accomplished skier without a well-developed ability to be aggressive when necessary.

For example, I recently worked with a friend who wanted to learn to ski steep slopes in control. He was experiencing a lack of ability to control his speed on steeper terrain. At the top of a steep slope, I asked him what he thought it would take to control his speed. He replied, "Well, I have to make turns where I don't gain speed with each turn." I asked him to make a series of comfortable turns, controlling his speed with each turn. He tried it, gained speed with each turn, and finally pulled to a stop. He was coasting, trying to repeat on this steep slope the same performance that he used on an easier slope.

He was not willing to become aggressive and control his speed with each turn.

I asked him what he thought it would take, other than technique, to control his speed. He thought about it again, and said, "I've got to be more aggressive." He tried it (he almost snarled with each turn!). His edges started holding, and his speed became more controlled with each turn. He realized the necessity of putting one hundred percent of his total energy into the control of his speed. He actually forgot his reasons for why he couldn't do it. Freed from mental distraction, he performed much more effectively. The experience was rewarding for him because, in those moments of aggressiveness, he found that he could ski better than he had originally thought.

We all have this ability, regardless of our level of accomplishment as skiers. It can be used when we are learning a new turn, skiing difficult snow, skiing a slalom course for the first time, or doing any movement that demands one hundred percent of our physical and mental output. Aggression takes us out of our minds into a state in which our body is capable of functioning at one hundred percent of its ability.

Efficient Movement

Being an accomplished skier requires efficient movement. Efficient movement is the ability to produce the desired result with a minimum amount of effort. Efficient movement allows you to operate at high speeds under difficult slope and snow conditions with surprising ease.

When I first learned to ski powder, I was told that it was necessary to unweight excessively in order to ski powder well. I followed this approach and noticed that I tired easily and had difficulty controlling my skis when I wanted to ski fast. I began to experiment with my movements in powder to see if I could eliminate some of my excessive unweighting. As I did, I found different ways to maneuver in powder, allowing me to ski faster and with less effort.

I applied this principle of eliminating inefficient movements to other aspects of my skiing. The results were very rewarding. I found that the more efficient the movement, the less energy it took to turn, to hold the edge, to carve turns, to ski at high speed, etc.

Begin looking at your skiing, and see where you can eliminate inefficient movements. As you do, you will begin to experience an increase in your energy and a continued increase in your ability to handle tough situations.

Complete Each Step Along the Way

Continue doing something until you know that you have completed every stage of it. For example, if you are learning to ski on gentle terrain, it is very unwise (and unhealthy) to attempt skiing on steeper terrain until *you know* you can handle the gentle stuff. First complete learning to ski on the gentle terrain, then move on to the next phase. If you move on to a new phase before you have completed the previous one, you will not be able to handle adequately the new phase. At some point in time, you will have to return and complete what you left undone.

When I went to Sun Valley to teach skiing, I really wanted to become an accomplished skier. I wanted to go to the top of the ski school ranks and immediately teach the most advanced students. However, the ski school director assigned me to beginners. At first I was very frustrated. I didn't feel that teaching beginners would assist me in becoming an accomplished skier.

I since have realized that he did me a great favor. He gave me the opportunity to learn completely how to teach beginning skiers. Through that process, I gained a tremendous amount of necessary experience and knowledge about how our bodies work on skis. Later I was able to apply that knowledge and experience directly to advanced skiing. Completing each step along the way will give you a sense of accomplishment and will totally prepare you for the next phase in your skiing.

6

Visualization

VISUALIZATION

When I first started skiing, I was a ski picture junkie. I collected everything I could find with a picture of a skier—books, magazines, posters, etc.—and studied them by the hour. First, I studied the pictures just for the fun of it. Later, I began to imagine that the figures on the page were moving, and finally, I started to imagine that I was the person in the photograph. I didn't realize it at the time, but I was using a very valid process for becoming an accomplished skier.

In this chapter there are a series of drawings that illustrate some of the basic movements in skiing. They are included for two reasons: first, to give you an example of the basic movements in skiing; and second, to give you a model for visualization exercises. When we look at drawings or photographs like these, our minds absorb what is on the page and even fill in details that aren't there. As our minds become increasingly familiar with a movement, through repeated observation, it is very easy to repeat that movement on snow.

Keep in mind that we are not presenting a finished form of how to ski. We are also not suggesting that these are the only movements in skiing or that you should do them precisely as they are drawn. These drawings are meant only for you to study and use as models for your own skiing. Allow your individualism to shine! Our bodies are different and have different ways of expressing motion. That's one of the beautiful things about skiing. We each create our own style and way of doing it.

Here's an exercise for making effective use of the drawings.

> *Pick one of the sequences that you would like to incorporate into your own skiing. Look at it. Do not try to figure it out or understand "how to do it." Just observe what is going on with the various figures on the page. Look at the track left by the skis. Look at the hands and posture of the figures in each part of the sequence you've chosen. Become totally familiar with all that is there in the sequence.*

> *Now, imagine the sequence coming alive, moving. Close your eyes, if that will help, and watch the figure move down the page. Imagine it in full color if you like (it's more entertaining that way). Let the sequence come alive.*

> *Next, imagine that the skier in the sequence is you. Picture yourself doing the movement. Allow yourself to become really confident. See yourself doing the movement from beginning to end.*

Pick up the book again a day later and repeat the entire exercise.

After a few days, create the mental images of yourself doing the sequence, without the book. Do this at a quiet moment so you can see yourself doing the entire sequence from beginning to end.

When you can recreate the whole thing in your mind without using the book, you're ready for the snow.

Remember that these drawings are only models for you to study. We are not suggesting that this is how you should look when you ski. You are different and you will look and ski differently from them. What you can gain from these drawings is a feeling for movements that work well in skiing, and then, if you choose, you can incorporate these movements into your own style of skiing.

Other sources for you to study are the current ski magazines (articles on technique, photos of skiers in advertisements), other books on skiing, and ski films—use them all.

VISUALIZATION

TRAVERSE

A traverse is the basic stance in skiing. Notice that it is an upright, relaxed stance, free from "positioning."

It is used for crossing or "traversing" a slope. The indicator of an effective traverse is the tracks left in the snow. When a traverse is effective, the tracks are distinct, unwavering, and parallel.

SNOWPLOW

The snowplow is the simplest form of controlling speed and changing direction of travel on skis. It is a necessarily skidded turn.

Spreading the tails of the skis while keeping the tips together creates a natural "plowing" attitude with the skis. Turning is accomplished by simply applying slightly more edge and pressure to one ski. The ski with more weight and edge will turn in the direction it is edged.

Snowplow braking and turning are effective at very slow speeds and in special situations such as traveling on a narrow trail where there is not room to create large radius turns.

ABSORB

This is the primary movement used by all skiers to absorb irregularities in terrain. The French use the word *avalement*, meaning "to swallow," for this movement. Proper absorption allows the body weight to remain over the feet at all times so the skier doesn't lose balance.

Efficient absorption happens when the skier allows the terrain to push his feet, legs, and hips up under him and then straighten on reaching level ground. The action is exactly the same as that of a car spring when a wheel passes over a bump in the road. The spring coils, allowing the wheel to pass over the bump, and then reacts by pushing the wheel back down on the road.

It is used by skiers of all levels of ability. It can be used while traversing, as shown here, while running straight down the hill, and it is used in all varieties of turns.

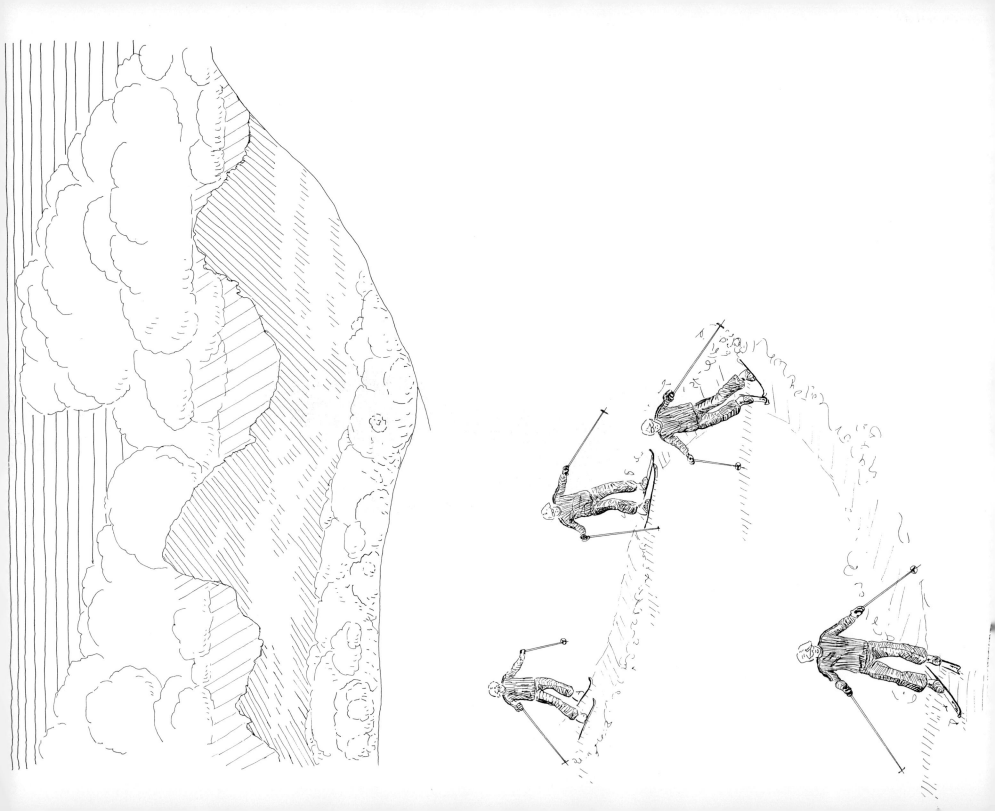

WIDE-TRACK TURN

Wide-track turns are the basic form of parallel skiing. They are skidded turns that are valuable for learning the coordination of edge-changing movements used in more advanced skiing.

There is no effort made to keep the skis running strictly parallel or tightly together. These turns are meant to be loose, easy, and fun.

They are used in the early stages of parallel skiing and can also be great exercise for "loosening up" the movements of more accomplished skiers.

RHYTHM

Rhythm is essential to all skiers, regardless of their level of ability. This sequence shows a series of unweighted parallel turns using a very regular rhythm. A skier employing this kind of rhythm can feel like the pendulum of a clock, moving with regularity and certainty from side to side.

Rhythm, however, need not always be regular. There can even be a rhythm within a rhythm. The use of rhythm among skiers is as widely varied as it is among musicians and their varieties of music.

Different rhythms are used by all accomplished skiers under all kinds of skiing conditions, including racing. Rhythm in skiing has the effect of greatly reducing the effort required to ski and allows the skier to move in greater harmony with the terrain.

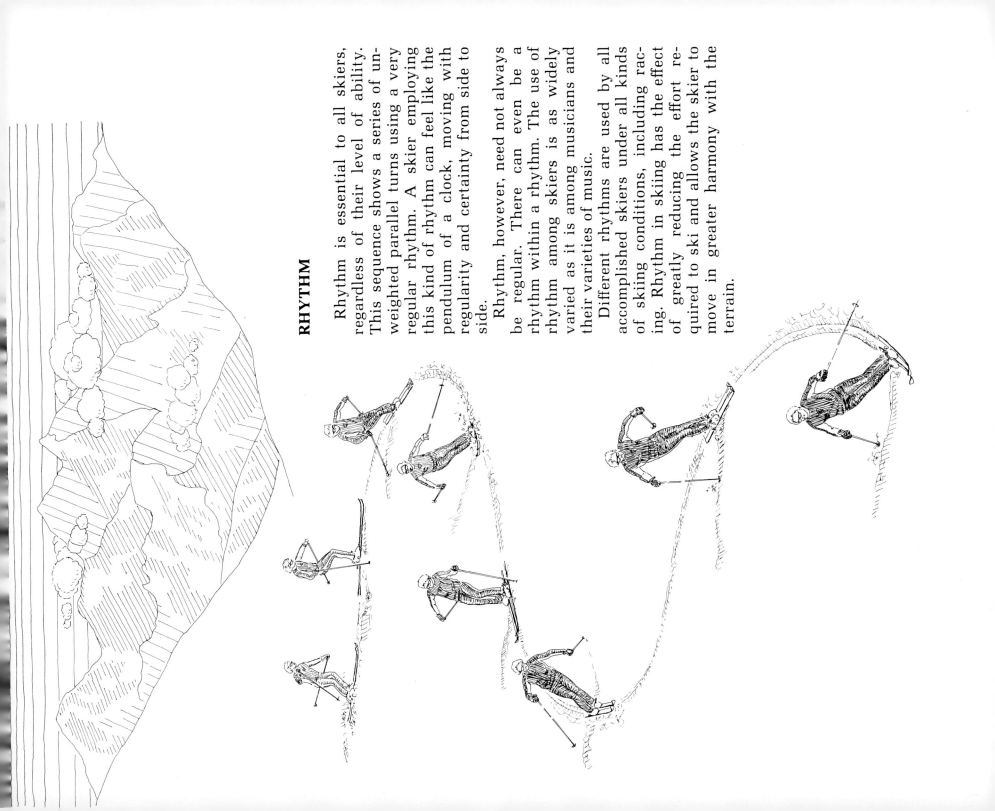

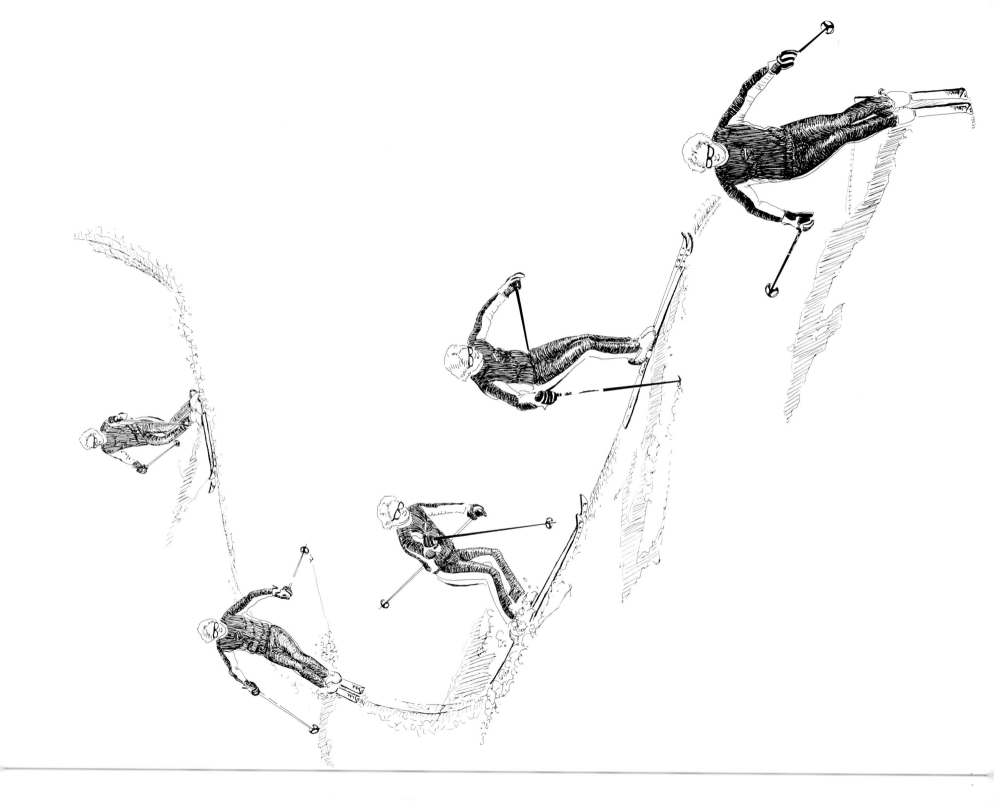

UNWEIGHTED PARALLEL TURN

An unweighted parallel turn is one of the primary turns in parallel skiing. It can be skidded or carved.

It is shown here with a check, used to create a platform for unweighting. The unweighting motion is used to create a distinct change of edges, thereby starting the skis carving in a new direction. The completion of the turns shown here is carved, as indicated by the tracks.

This and other forms of unweighted parallel turns are used by skiers of all levels of ability under all skiing conditions—powder, hard pack, moguls, racing, etc.

STEP TURN

A step turn is a turn in which the initiation and edge change is accomplished by stepping from the downhill ski to the uphill ski and then proceeding to turn. It gives the skier the advantage of creating early edging and a long, carving turn with maximum control.

It is a very good exercise for developing independent leg action, a highly developed ability of all accomplished skiers. It is used very effectively in slalom and giant slalom racing, high-speed free skiing, and mogul skiing, and it is an excellent way to recover from a momentary loss of balance.

ABSORB TURN

This is a parallel turn in which the edges are changed as the body achieves momentary weightlessness on top of the mogul. It can be a particularly effortless method of turning because the skier is making use of natural unweighting as his body passes over terrain irregularities.

It can be a skidded or carved turn. The turn shown here is carved as indicated by the tracks. Notice that the body weight remains effectively over the feet during the entire turn.

This turn is used by skiers of all levels of ability. It is particularly useful on heavily moguled slopes. Very creative variations of this turn are used on race courses and in powder and crud skiing.

STEEP

In order to create stability and control on skis, every skier must keep his upper body weight constantly over his skis when they are in effective contact with the snow. This is particularly important on steeper slopes.

This sequence illustrates this simple, and highly important, rule: When skiing steep terrain, keep your upper body perpendicular to the slope you are skiing on. The sensation a skier experiences is one of pushing more forward in the boots as the slope increases in steepness.

The result of keeping your body weight over your feet is maintaining constant, effective control over your skis.

REBOUND

Rebound is using the momentum of your body rather than muscle effort to create an edge change and turn initiation.

A skier moving at fast speed can use his momentum to create an impact against the snow that actually bounces him from one turn to the next. The effect is exactly the same as bouncing a basketball against the floor. When the ball impacts against the floor, it reacts by rebounding away from the floor.

It is an extremely quick, effortless, and efficient method of initiating turns. It is used by all accomplished skiers and is particularly effective in moguls, on race courses, and on icy slopes.

EARLY EDGING

Early edging is accomplished by placing the skis on edge and weighting them *before* they enter the fall line. This gives the skier the added advantage of controlling his speed early in the turn and then continuing a normal carved turn.

Edging and weighting skis early can be accomplished with any kind of turn initiation and gives the skier the ability to control his rate of acceleration during the turn. The effect is the same as driving a car through a turn. Slowing down as the car enters the turn allows the driver to accelerate with control coming out of the turn.

This ability is employed by *all* accomplished skiers in all skiing conditions, i.e., racing, ice, steep slopes, powder, moguls, etc.

POWDER/CRUD

The basic stance on skis does not need to alter dramatically under any snow or slope condition. This sequence of turns in powder might just as well have been illustrated in crud snow conditions; you would see no alteration in the skier's stance or movement.

The only thing necessary to initiate turns in powder or crud is to momentarily break the resistance of the deep snow. This can be accomplished through any form of turn initiation, the most effective being shown here.

Notice that, once the turn is initiated, normal carving is used to complete the turn.

Skiing powder snow is one of the most thrilling experiences in skiing and is surprisingly easy to master.

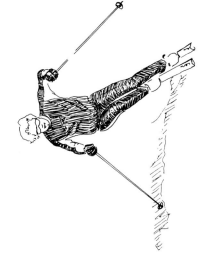

ICE

Skiing ice is a game of creating maximum resistance between your skis and the ice/snow.

The most effective skills used in skiing ice are shown here: early edging; concentrating all the weight on the turning ski (notice the lifted ski with each turn); applying maximum edge and weight on the turning ski during the center of each turn; and stepping between turns to initiate each turn.

Skiing ice is extremely creative. Accomplished skiers also use terrain to great advantage when skiing ice, i.e., breaking speed against moguls, turning on spots where there is no ice, etc.

MOGULS

The top mogul and free skiers are extremely inventive in their approach to skiing bumps. They will use *any* kind of turn or balancing stunt to get the job done. When a skier has this attitude, a field of moguls becomes a giant playground.

The most effective forms of turning in moguls are shown here and are listed in the same order as they appear on the sequential drawing: short carving (and skidded) turns with a sudden check at the bottom of the turn; an unweighted parallel turn; banking; a step turn; an absorption turn; a long, shallow carved turn between moguls; and an airplane turn (using a mogul to become airborne in order to clear rough ground between bumps).

This variety of turns and creativity is the key to all accomplished mogul skiing.

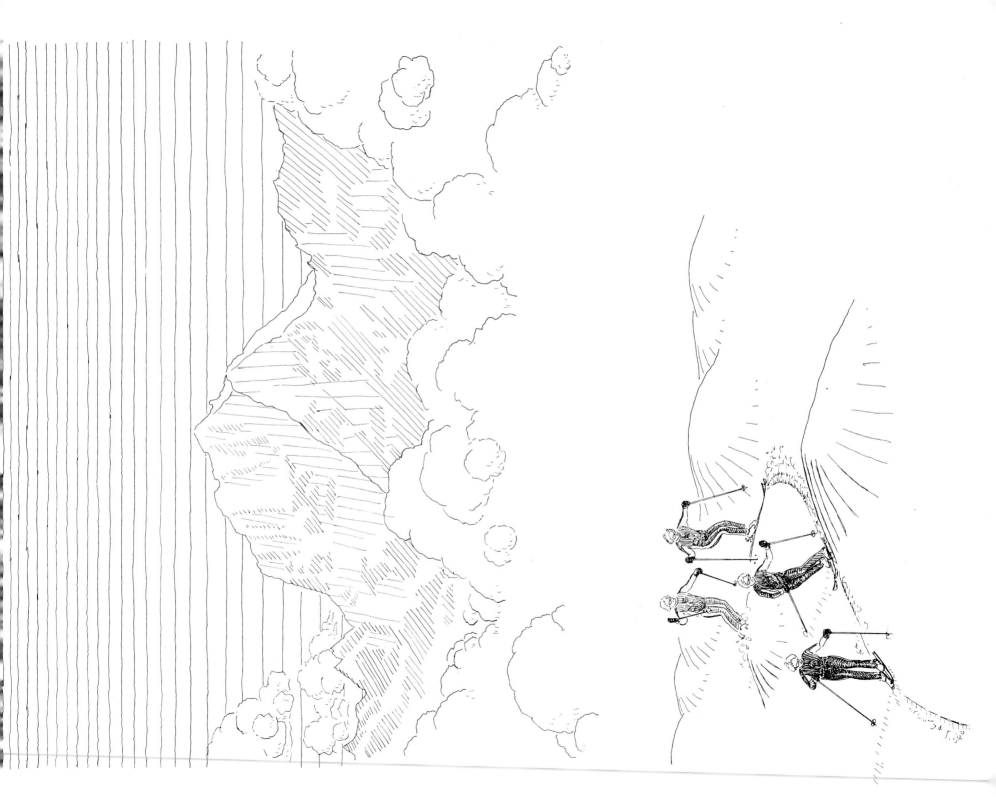

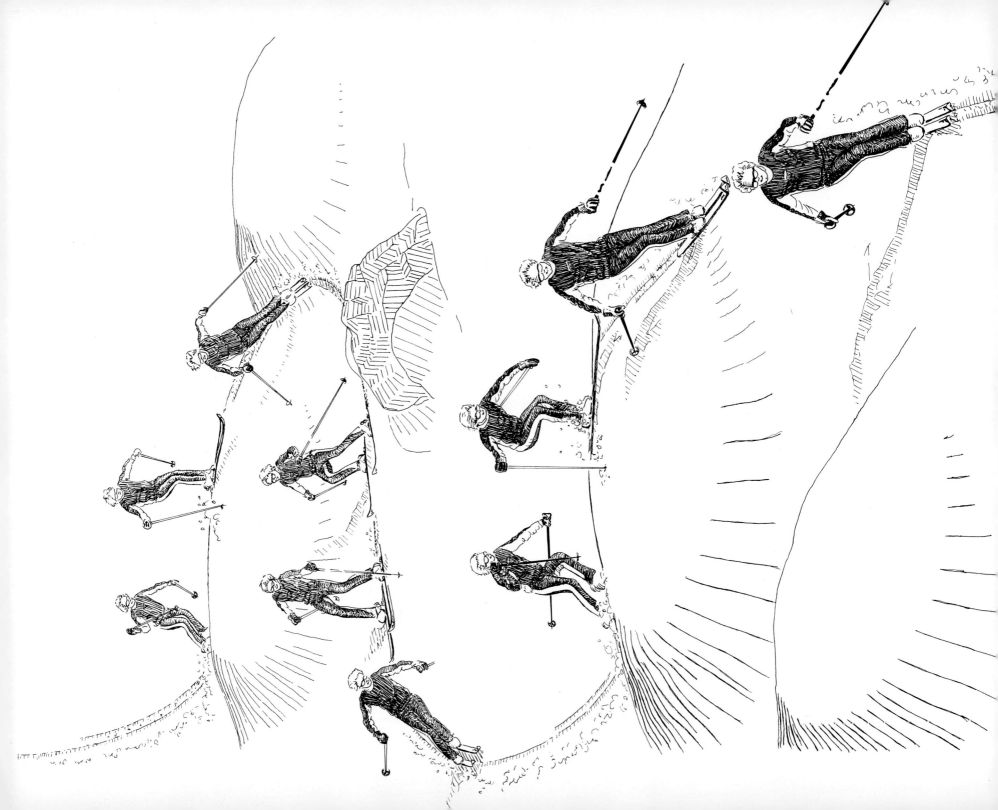

7

The Hidden Skier

by Christopher Smith

THE HIDDEN SKIER

Each time you learn something new while skiing, you experience the "Hidden Skier" within you. I am referring to it as "hidden" because it is already there as a part of you, yet it may not always appear to be there. The more you ski, the more you will develop and easily recognize that skier within yourself.

If you are a very accomplished skier, you are experiencing that skier to a very high degree. If you are a beginner, or somewhat accomplished, yet cannot seem to progress any further, you may wonder if it exists at all in you. Yet, all accomplished skiers had to start out as and look like beginners at one time. They continued developing themselves until they experienced what they wanted of themselves as skiers.

There may be times when it does not look as though you have what it takes to learn to ski a particular run. Whatever your reasons are, *don't believe them.* If you give up and believe your reasons for why you cannot do something, you won't be able to do it. The mountain won't be stopping you, your "lack of ability" won't be stopping you, *you* will be stopping you. If you are not progressing in the manner you think you should, it does not mean that you are untalented. It only means that's how you are progressing right now. It does not indicate how you will progress in the future.

The natural process of learning takes place as we *do* whatever it is we want to learn. It does not happen through someone telling us "how to do it." Becoming accomplished at something happens by our *continuing to do* that something, as well as our seeing ourselves as becoming accomplished.

You aren't adding on to yourself when you learn something new. You can't do that; you are already complete as you are. What you are doing is adjusting and developing the movements you already have so they will successfully accomplish what you want to do. You're subtracting your inefficient movements by making them efficient.

When you "fail" at learning something new, you are simply experiencing some of your inefficient and unworkable movements. It is part of your natural process. You are simply allowing yourself to see which movements need to be made more efficient so you can succeed. As you continue doing what you want to learn, your inefficient movements will become more efficient, naturally. It doesn't matter what you look like, or how slow or fast you learn things; everyone has the capacity to improve his or her physical performance. The only real barrier that will stop you is thinking you cannot do it.

If you want to accelerate your learning process in skiing, and at the same time have fun with it, you can. Improving your skiing does not have to be accomplished with hard work and effort.

The first place to start is with your thoughts. Neutralize your negative thoughts and create positive ones that help you to develop your skiing, not hinder it. Then create an approach to skiing on the snow that will make it fun, and at the same time, develop the basic elements of skiing within your own style of skiing. All of the chapters in the book preceding this one have given you specific ways to accomplish this.

Everything Corky and I have presented has been out of our own experience both as athletes and teachers. We've seen that becoming an accomplished skier is easy to do; in fact, becoming an accomplished athlete in any sport is easy to do.

The Hidden Athlete Workshop is the living version of this book, as Corky mentioned in the Introduction. The results the workshop has produced have been part of the research that has gone into this book. We've seen people of all ages, from twelve to sixty, be able to improve their athletic performance, not by changing their instructor, but rather by changing their attitudes about what they thought they were capable of doing. More impressive yet was that they had more fun and were much more relaxed about what they were doing.

Doing sports like skiing, tennis, swimming, basketball, etc., have been the areas in my life in which I've experienced the most fun and growth. They're always exciting, especially when I can share the experience with someone else.

Writing this book actually started a year and a half before I met Corky. I was a tennis pro in Los Angeles where I created a program of teaching based on my own experiences of learning, which centered around my positive attitude about what I could do as an athlete and having fun at whatever I did.

Not only was the program successful, but I also realized that what I was saying had to do with any sport, not just tennis.

While teaching tennis during the summer, I was skiing every winter, spending four winters in Europe. I found that skiing was also very easy to learn, yet there were a lot of people who did not share my feelings. They were working at it rather than having fun with it.

I met Corky through mutual friends two winters ago and found that he felt exactly as I did about learning sports, especially skiing. He also noticed that a lot of people did not share the ease of learning skiing that we did. We decided to write a book, one that would make skiing easier and more fun for anyone. We did and it has been an incredible experience for both of us.

The purpose of this book is to communicate a process through which anyone can learn or improve his skiing and, at the same time, enjoy himself. You can take the mental approach we've presented here and apply it to any sport, or anywhere in life for that matter. It is all the same thing.

THE HIDDEN SKIER

As easily as I have been able to learn sports, there have been periods of time when I had to work very hard at learning something, only to find out that I could have learned it in a different way. A way in which I exerted less energy and accomplished more. I had one of those experiences a while back with Corky, who is one of the most accomplished skiers I've ever seen. I was trying to improve my skiing and was working on it every day. One day he said, "Come with me. I want to show you something I used to do all the time in Sun Valley." We did something I had never done before. We skied very long distances without stopping. It was incredible. I was skiing so fast that I never even thought about what I was doing. I didn't have time! I enjoyed myself so much that I skied with him for four more days in a row, doing the same thing. Each day we skied a little faster and a little farther.

I found that experience to be so valuable to my skiing that now I ski "just to ski" most of the time. If I want to work with a particular aspect of my skiing, I spend a specific amount of time doing that and then return to skiing for the fun of it.

I cannot express this point strongly enough. **If you want to improve your skiing, it is extremely important that you spend a significant amount of time just skiing for the pure joy of skiing.**

It's up to you at this point. All books, including this one, are full of concepts and printed words, but they won't ski for you. You can, however, take the experiences communicated here and make them your own.

Your experience of skiing is what counts, make it what you want it to be. . . .